P9-DFR-303

THE OFFICE OF

The Scarlet Letter

Parallax: Re-visions of Culture and Society

Stephen G. Nichols, Gerald Prince, and Wendy Steiner, Series Editors

THE OFFICE OF
The Scarlet Letter

Sacvan Bercovitch

THE JOHNS HOPKINS UNIVERSITY PRESS
BALTIMORE AND LONDON

The Johns Hopkins University Press
701 West 40th Street
Baltimore, Maryland 21211
The Johns Hopkins Press Ltd., London

∞ The paper used in this book meets the minimum requirements of American National Standard for Information Sciences—Permanence of Paper for Printed Library Materials, ANSI Z39.48-1984.

LIBRARY OF CONGRESS CATALOGING-IN-PUBLICATION DATA

Bercovitch, Sacvan.
The office of The scarlet letter / Sacvan Bercovitch.
p. cm. – (Parallax : re-visions of culture and society)
Includes bibliographical references and index.
ISBN 0-8018-4203-4 (alk. paper)
1. Hawthorne, Nathaniel, 1804–1864. Scarlet letter. I. Title.
II. Series: Parallax (Baltimore, Md.)
PS1868.B395 1991
813′.3—dc20 90-25798
CIP

Contents

To Susan

Acknowledgments

PART OF THE MATERIALS here were first presented as the Troy Lectures at the University of Massachusetts, Amherst. Two of the lectures were published, in different form, in *New Literary History* and *Representations.* The book itself was completed at the Woodrow Wilson International Center for Scholars. I want to express my gratitude for the extraordinary intellectual forum provided in each case and to thank friends and colleagues who offered encouragement and criticism. I also want to express my gratitude to my research assistant, Margaret Reid. My greatest debt particularly is to Eytan Bercovitch.

Introduction

"THE SCARLET LETTER had not done its office": Hawthorne's stern, evasive one-line paragraph, midway through the novel, deserves the emphasis he gives it.[1] The sentence links our various views of Hester Prynne—on the pillory and in the forest, in relation to the townspeople, her husband, her lover, her daughter, herself. It seems to confirm what we are often told, that Hawthorne's meanings are endless and open-ended. To speak of an office not done, especially without specifying the office, implies a commitment to process, a principled indefiniteness. But in fact Hawthorne is saying just the opposite. His very emphasis on the negative, the "not done," invests the letter with a discrete function, an office whose fulfillment (in due time) will be the mark of narrative closure. It reminds us, as does everything else about the novel, from title to plot, that the letter has a purpose and a goal. And to speak of an unfulfilled office when fulfillment is under way, not *yet* done, is to imply teleology. Hawthorne's meanings may be endless, but they are not open-ended. On the contrary, they are designed to create a specific set of anticipations, to shape our understanding of what follows in some definite way.

"The scarlet letter had not done its office": on one hand, process; on the other hand, purpose and telos. The coherence of the symbol lies in its capacity to combine both. It has a certain end, we might say, in the double sense of "certain," as certainty and as something still to be ascertained. The office of the letter is to identify one with the other—to make certainty a form of process, and the prospect of certain meanings a form of closure and control.

With that double prospect in view, Hester returns to New England. "Here had been her sin," Hawthorne writes, "here, her sorrow; and here was yet to be her penitence" (344). Again, process and closure have been combined, only now with a *certain* end in view—penitence—as earlier Dimmesdale has an end in view when he prophesies a certain "glorious destiny" for "this newly chosen people of the Lord" (332–33) and as Hester does later when she foresees an age of love to come. Once, long before, she transformed the A into a symbol for able, admirable. Now she transforms herself, able and admirable as she is, into an agent of socialization. Her cottage becomes a meeting ground for dissidents—particularly, unhappy young women chafing (as Hester had) under Puritan restrictions—and she takes the opportunity to make it a counseling center for patience and faith. In effect, she urges upon them a morphology of penitence (not unlike the official Puritan "preparation for salvation"): self-control, self-doubt, self-denial, a true sight of sin, and hope in the future, involving some apodictic revelation to come. Hester's "badge of shame" becomes the "mystic" token of integration (257, 146).

This is not some formulaic Victorian happy ending. In the first place, the ending is not happy. What brings Hester home, the necessity that serves in some measure (as Hawthorne promises at the start) to "relieve the darkening close" of his tale (159), is no deus ex machina. It is the narrative mechanism itself, in all its "sad" and "sombre" implications (345). Hawthorne sums them up through the emblem on the lovers' tombstone—the "engraved escutcheon . . . relieved by one ever-glowing point of light gloomier than the shadow" (345)—an emblem that enforces our sense of closure precisely by sustaining narrative tension, for, like Hester's final penitence to be, the gloom that finally is to provide relief also returns us to the ambiguities of Hester's ordeal.

In these and other ways, Hawthorne's fusion of process and telos transmutes opposition into complementarity. Hester's return effectually reconciles the various antinomies that surround her throughout the novel: nature and culture, sacred and profane, light and shadow, memory and hope, repression and desire, angel and adulteress, her dream of love and the demands of history and community. It also draws together author and subject, for, as the letter's unfulfilled office midway through the story anticipates Hester's return, so the return of Hester anticipates Hawthorne's recovery of Puritan New England. Here had been her penitence, and here was yet to be *The Scarlet Letter: A Romance*. At the start Hawthorne reverses the disruptive effects of political office—the Democratic party defeat that cost him his tenure at the Salem Customs House—by reaching back through the A to national origins. At the end, reversing the alienating effects of her symbol, Hester looks forward to a "brighter period" (344) that relates her most intimate hopes to moral and social progress. In each case, the gesture enacts the symbolic method I noted, process and telos combined. And in each case the method reflects the strategies of what we have come to term "the American ideology."

The term requires a more precise definition, which I will elaborate, but, even in its vague implications—pertaining to the norms of the dominant culture—ideology, as Hawthorne suggests, is a rich and intricate system of meanings. *The Scarlet Letter* is a story of socialization in which the point of socialization is not to conform, but to consent. Anyone can submit; the socialized believe. It is not enough to have the letter imposed; you have to do it yourself, and that involves the total self—past, present, and future; private and public; thought and passion and action, or, if necessary, inaction. This is essentially the office of the A as the Puritan magistrates intended it and as Hester finally adopts it, from her own far more tolerant but not altogether different outlook. And we can assume that the letter's "deeper meanings" correspond. *Allegoria,* as Saint Augustine taught, is a function of *littera-historia.* By that time-honored principle of exegesis, the A is first and last a cultural artifact, a symbol that expresses the needs of the society within and for which it was produced. I refer to Hawthorne's society, of course, but I would also include Puritan New England, insofar as it may be said to have contributed to the development of antebellum ideology, and our period as well, insofar as it may be said to build on ideological continuities from Hawthorne's time.

By "Hawthorne's society" and "antebellum ideology" I mean the complex of social practices and cultural ideals that we associate with the liberal Northern United States from 1820 to the Civil War. I am aware of the many differences within that society and of the many problems in applying such generalities as "Jacksonian" to the Northern states. My concern lies with the broad patterns of life and thought that nonetheless bound together those diverse interests, groups, and regions (as events demonstrated), and within which, moreover, diversity itself was celebrated as part of a strategy of cultural cohesion. As an anticonsensus historian reports in a survey of the scholarship: "the recent literature argues that politicians and lawmakers of all persuasions (including southern politicians . . .) were becoming increasingly enamored of liberal concepts . . . [and] came increasingly to interpret the republican framework as one or another form of liberal capitalist polity and economy." This study is in part a commentary on that engulfing process of interpretation—a process, let me add, that reaches back to "the republican framework." "The name of AMERICAN," said George Washington in his Farewell Address (September 17, 1796), "must always exalt [your] just pride . . . more than any appellation derived from local discriminations. With slight shades of difference, you have the same Religion, Manners, Habits, and political Principles."[2]

The "name of AMERICAN" was an interpretative fiction in 1796 no less than it was in 1776 (or for that matter two centuries earlier, when it had served the opposite-but-complementary office of interpreting away differences between the religions, manners, habits, and political principles of the peoples we now again call Native Americans). But by mid-century it had become the cornerstone of a New World liberal identity that extended from the free enterprise vision of "American Economy" to the multidenominational varieties of "American Religion," and that included the "Shiloh" mission of "Young America in Literature," which Melville in 1850 ascribed to Hawthorne.[3] In all this the name of American worked not only to displace the very real (and deepening) differences within the country, but equally—within the country's reigning liberal constituency—to display difference of all kinds as proof of a victorious pluralism. The result was a quasi-dialectic between exclusion and expansion that established, defined, and processually secured the boundaries of union, a "new nation" replete with mythic past and "manifest" future. Hawthorne and his contemporaries traced this cultural genealogy to Puritan New England, as did many of the leaders of both revolutionary and republican America. Their rhetoric of descent (simultaneously a rhetoric of ascent and consent) is central to the dynamics of cohesion in the movement from republican to Jacksonian America.

The scarlet letter functions in this sense as cultural genealogy; it functions, too, as it moves from the mid-nineteenth-century customshouse back to its Puritan origins, to recall a major cultural shift from "civic" to individualistic norms. Historians have described this shift in conflictual terms, as entailing massive realignments of social, economic, and regional power. I am indebted to their descriptions, as the following chapters testify. My own focus, however, lies elsewhere—on the forces that recast conflict and change (potentially, the sort of radical upheavals that virtually everywhere else, in both the Old World and the New, led to the collapse of liberal revolutions) into a triumph of the American ideology. I have in mind the sustained liberal commitment of those who spoke for the Republic: the shared values, symbols, and beliefs that at once fueled and circumscribed the debates between Thomas Jefferson and John Adams, Thomas Paine and Timothy Dwight, Andrew Jackson and John Quincy Adams, Ralph Waldo Emerson and Daniel Webster, Abraham Lincoln and Stephen Douglas. Those debates can be said to mark the organic development from "classical" to "marketplace" liberalism. And in turn that quintessentially ideological development can be said to have guided the nation, through a civil war of unprecedented violence and destruction, from the era of liberal expansion to that of liberal incorporation.

I use "liberal" here and throughout this study as a catchall term to convey the continuing relation between social process and cultural symbology. In doing so, I dispute neither the technical social scientific sense of the term, as in Theodore Lowi's thesis about "the end of liberalism" under Franklin Delano Roosevelt's New Deal, nor its specific philosophical import, as in Michael Sandel's explication of "the limitations of justice" in liberal thought. On the contrary, my assumption is that all those centripetal distinctions support the argument for continuity—and nowhere more clearly, I believe, than in the current rhetorical battles between "conservatives," quoting Jefferson, John Adams, Tom Paine, Emerson, Lincoln, and Roosevelt, and advocates of the "L-word," such as People for the American Way and the American Civil Liberties Union. Academic specialists who seize upon the (abundant) inconsistencies in these polemics would do well to recall Walt Whitman's epic response to such charges: the American Self can contain multitudes.[4] As we shall see, that strategy of containment, together with the concept of representative individualism it implies, could also elicit (as in Hester Prynne) the paradoxical dynamics of dissent.

In this long view the office of the scarlet letter pertains both to the symbol in the text and to the symbol as the text. My purpose, accordingly, is to integrate ideological and aesthetic criticism. Ideology in its narrow sense works to empty objects of historical content—particularly, in our time, objects of art. It depoliticizes them in order to refill them with its own timeless and universal claims. I want to repoliticize *The Scarlet Letter* (in Aristotle's broad sense of the political) by turning the text inside out and the context outside in: to explain the novel's aesthetic design in terms of cultural strategies of control and to allow the culture to reveal itself in all its radical potentiality through its representation in the text.

Hence my emphasis on what I call, for lack of a better term, cultural symbology. I mean by it neither the "superstructures" posited by social science (where "ideology" is synonymous with false consciousness or *parti pris*) nor the fabled realm of the transcendent (our post-Romantic kingdom of God)—but the system of symbolic meanings that encompasses text and context alike, simultaneously nourishing the imagination and marking its boundaries. It is a highly volatile system, built upon multilayered connections between dominant patterns of cultural expression and their distinctive uses in exceptional works of art, as Hester's exotic letter connects to a wide range of Puritan *canonica*, from the Pentateuch to the illustrated catechism of the New England primer. Cultural symbology at once denies aesthetic autonomy and highlights the difference between aesthetics and the political or institutional forms usually associated with ideology. It reminds us that aesthetic representations are inescapably political, just as literature necessarily assumes an institutional form. It also reminds us that they are flexible enough to accommodate upheaval and transformation, that this flexibility may extend in extraordinary cases across time and place, and that, at a certain pitch of intensity, this transhistorical appeal may become the vehicle not only of elusiveness and indeterminacy but also of personal agency and social subversion.

The model I have in mind is, of course, the scarlet letter itself. The terms in which I just outlined its office as cultural work are intended in the loose sense of practical criticism—what might be called an ethnography of literary context. The boundaries I refer to include cross-cultural influences and conflicting modes of expression and belief. Their relation to ideology is variable and possibly disruptive. Ideology itself, in the anthropological sense I intend, involves a network of complex reciprocities between social construction and textual creation. And although I assume a basic contextual coherence—a system within which such terms as "cross-cultural," "conflicting," and "variable" make sense—I do so primarily by reference to a singular symbolic work of art. My point is not to demystify *The Scarlet Letter.* It is to call into question—that is, to problematize so as to seek knowledge from—its extraordinary powers of mystification. To understand the novel historically is to recognize that we learn most about background and sources from its aesthetic techniques. And to appreciate it aesthetically is to recognize that what is richest and most compelling about the novel lies in its profound ideological engagement—profound enough to allow us to trace the issues it masks; ideologically engaged enough to have made this darkest of Hawthorne's novels (as it has often been described) a vehicle of continuity at a time of cultural disruption and social change.

I think here not only of the continuities inscribed in the novel, from Puritan to antebellum New England and beyond, but of the widespread response to *The Scarlet Letter.* From the start readers acclaimed the novel for its representative national qualities. "Our literature has given the world no truer product of the American soil," declared Young America's literary pundit, Evert Duyckinck, upon the novel's appearance in 1850, and in one form or another his judgment was echoed by virtually every important nineteenth-century critic through William

Dean Howells and Duyckinck's Gilded Age successor, the Brahmin literary entrepreneur Horace Scudder. It is not too much to say that *The Scarlet Letter* began the institutionalization of an American literary tradition. Of the three "immortals" officially enshrined in 1900 as the founders of American literature—Washington Irving, Henry Wadsworth Longfellow, and Hawthorne—only Hawthorne survived the twentieth-century revaluation of the canon. And of the several books that contemporaries singled out as his masterpiece—*Mosses from an Old Manse, The Scarlet Letter, The House of the Seven Gables,* and *The Marble Faun*—only *The Scarlet Letter,* our first instant classic, has retained its appeal for subsequent generations of readers.[5]

It is worth emphasizing the political import of this process. At mid-century Hawthorne's novel was the chief authority by which the new nation claimed independence in the realm of belles lettres. It "represented both what was essentially American," according to contemporary reviewers, "and what was 'best' by . . . universal criteria." By the turn of the century *The Scarlet Letter* was the centerpiece in the "general incorporation of literature into education," as expressing the "national spirit" in its "consummate" form—"the embodiment of what Americans share, the chief incarnation of the ethos that gives them existence as people . . . [and therefore for educational purposes,] the channel through which that ethos is disseminated, and . . . the means by which outsiders are brought inside it."[6]

The apotheosis of that tradition-making rite of passage came with Henry James's biography of 1879, which celebrates Hawthorne as "the most valuable example of the American genius." *The Scarlet Letter,* writes James, is

> the finest piece of imaginative writing yet put forth in the country. There was a consciousness of this in the welcome that was given it—a satisfaction in the idea of America having produced a novel that belonged to literature, and to the forefront of it. Something might at last be sent to Europe as exquisite in quality as anything that had been

received, and the best of it was that the thing was absolutely American. . . . [Hawthorne remains] the writer to whom his countrymen most confidently point when they wish to make a claim to have enriched the mother tongue . . . [and *The Scarlet Letter*] will continue to be, for other generations than ours, his most substantial title to fame.

James's acclaim was the elite mark of sanctification. The broad consensus to which he refers—reaching backward to the novel's first "welcome" and forward to its future "fame"—was being systematically enlarged throughout this time by an intricate network of belletristic, social, and economic institutions, including publishing houses, political and cultural reviews, salons, home libraries, public events, university lectures, and high school texts.[7]

These facts do not point toward a conspiracy theory of canon formation. Nor do they imply that literature is a form of co-optation. They suggest that the power of the text, in all its extraordinary intensity and multivalence, is inseparable from context and function. Culture works through a variety of agencies, forces, and pressures, some of these mutually contradictory. But basically it seeks to perpetuate itself through strategies of cohesion, and (in modern instances) it does so most effectively through particular rhetorical forms, designed to instate particular sets of norms and beliefs.

Literature participates in this design. It is nourished by the same values, sustained by the same institutions, and informed by the same codes of personal and communal identity through which culture works. In the case of *The Scarlet Letter*—as in that of all our mid-nineteenth-century classics, including Harriet Beecher Stowe's *Uncle Tom's Cabin* (1851–52) and Frederick Douglass's *The Narrative of the Life of Frederick Douglass* (1845)—the source of that reciprocity may be simply stated. It lies in the premises of American liberalism: "America," a national symbol denoting not only a national identity (as in Washington's Farewell Address) but also a literary ideal, and "liberalism," an interpretative framework denoting not only general habits of the heart and mind but also a particular economy, free enterprise capitalism in the antebellum North. Let me recall the powerful link between the two. "America" is to New World liberalism as the doctrine of the divine right of kings is to medieval monarchy. Open competition, group pluralism, voluntarism, private enterprise, personal rights, community by contract and consent, equality under the law, mobility, free opportunity, individualism—all the tenets of modern liberal society find their apotheosis in the symbol of America. The process by which the United States usurped America for itself, symbolically, is also the process by which liberalism established its political and economic dominance.

This double process took effect between the Revolution and the Civil War, and its aesthetic triumph is marked by the American literary renaissance. The locus classicus is 1850, the year of *The Scarlet Letter*—also of Susan Warner's *Wide, Wide World*, our amplest inside narrative of liberal domesticity, and Herman Melville's *Moby-Dick*, still the most searching critique we have of free enterprise democracy.* Of these, Hawthorne's novel is the prime instance of literature as cultural work. It represents not only a set of ideologically mediated realities but also the ways and means of mediation. To some extent this is true of the other two novels as well, but each of them stands in a relatively tangential relation to society: Warner's by defini-

*In a separate, much broader work, concerning the development of liberal institutions in antebellum America (including the institution of literature), I explore these and other texts as complementary, conflicting, or alternative sites of culture formation and/or cultural critique. In doing so, I take up aspects of Hawthorne's writing that are treated here only in passing: for example, issues of gender (as in Warner's novel) and varieties of countercultural work (in the tradition of Melville). *The Scarlet Letter* has been used to discuss these concerns, most recently and most fully from a feminist perspective in important book-length studies (forthcoming) by Lauren Berlant and Emily Budick. My present purpose is to offer *within the author's frame of discourse* a certain kind of contextual close reading—that is, a cultural *explication de texte* in which ideological analysis is a form of "intrinsic criticism," and vice versa.

tion of "the woman's sphere" and Melville's because of his profoundly marginal perspective. *The Scarlet Letter* has proved our most enduring classic because it is the liberal example par excellence of art as ideological mimesis. To understand the office of the A, to appreciate its subtle combinings of process and closure, is to see how culture empowers symbolic form, including forms of dissent, and how symbols participate in the dynamics of culture, including the dynamics of constraint. In what follows I explore these connections from two perspectives, each of them interchangeably textual and contextual: first, a historical reading of the novel's unities (chapters 1 and 2); and then, a rhetorical analysis of certain key mid-nineteenth-century issues, at home and abroad (chapters 3 and 4). And in order to highlight the relation between rhetoric and history, I focus on the point at which the scarlet letter does its office at last, the dramatic moment when Hester decides to come home to America.

THE OFFICE OF *The Scarlet Letter*

Chapter One

The A-Politics of Ambiguity

THE DRAMA OF Hester Prynne's return has gone unappreciated, no doubt because it is absent from the novel. At a certain missing point in the narrative, through an unrecorded process of introspection, Hester abandons the high, sustained self-reliance by which we have come to identify her, from her opening gesture of defiance, when she repels the beadle and walks proudly "into the open air" (162), to the forest scene seven years later, when she casts off her A and urges Dimmesdale to a new life—choosing for no clear reason to abandon her heroic independence and acquiescing to the A after all. Voluntarily she returns to the colony that had tried to make her (she once believed) a "life-long bond-slave," although Hawthorne pointedly records the rumors that Pearl "would most joyfully have entertained [her] . . . mother at her fireside" (313–14, 344). And voluntarily Hester resumes the letter as a "woman stained with sin, bowed down with shame," although, he adds, "not the sternest magistrate of that iron period would have imposed it" (344). As in a camera obscura, isolation and schism are inverted into vehicles of moral, political, and historical continuity:

> Women, more especially . . . came to Hester's cottage, demanding why they were so wretched, and what the remedy! Hester comforted and counseled them, as best she might. She assured them, too, of her

firm belief, that, at some brighter period, when the world should have grown ripe for it, in Heaven's own time, a new truth would be revealed, in order to establish the whole relation between man and woman on a surer ground of mutual happiness. Earlier in life, Hester had vainly imagined that she herself might be the destined prophetess, but had long since recognized the impossibility that any mission of divine and mysterious truth should be confided to a woman stained with sin, bowed down with shame, or even burdened with a life-long sorrow. The angel and apostle of the coming revelation must be a woman, indeed, but lofty, pure, and beautiful; and wise, moreover, not through dusky grief, but the ethereal medium of joy; and showing how sacred love should make us happy, by the truest test of a life successful to such an end! (344–45)

The entire novel tends toward this moment of reconciliation, but the basis for reconciliation, the source of Hester's revision, remains entirely unexplained. The issue is not that Hester returns, which Hawthorne does account for, in his way: "There was a more real life for Hester Prynne, here, in New England" (344). Nor is it that she resumes the A: we might anticipate that return to beginnings, by the principles of narrative closure. What remains problematic, what Hawthorne compels us to explain for ourselves (as well as on Hester's behalf), is her dramatic change of purpose and belief. Throughout her "seven years of outlaw and ignominy," Hester had considered her A a "scorching stigma" and herself "the people's victim" (331, 291, 313–14). Only some "galling" combination of fatalism and love, Hawthorne tells us early in the novel, had kept her from leaving the colony at once, after her condemnation (188). She had been "free to return" to England; she had also had

the passes of the dark, inscrutable forest open to her, where the wildness of her nature might assimilate itself with a people whose customs and life were alien from the law that had condemned her. . . . But [Hester was possessed by] . . . a fatality, a feeling so irresistible and inevitable that it ha[d] the force of doom. . . . Her sin, her ignominy, were the roots which she had struck into the soil. It was as if a new birth, with stronger assimilations than the first, had converted the forest-land . . . into Hester Prynne's wild and dreary, but life-long home. . . . The chain that bound her here was of iron links, and galling to her inmost soul. . . . What she compelled herself to believe,—what, finally, she reasoned upon, as her motive for continuing a resident of New England,—was half a truth, and half a self-delusion. Here, she said to herself, had been the scene of her guilt, and here should be the scene of her daily punishment; and so, perchance, the torture of her daily shame would at length purge her soul, and work out another purity than that which she had lost; more saint-like, because the result of martyrdom. (186–87)

Something of that force of necessity attends Hester's return, together with that earlier self-denying, self-aggrandizing quest for martyrdom. But it now conveys a far less "wild and dreary" prospect. Hester chooses to make herself not only an object of the law, "saint-like" by her resignation to "daily punishment," but more largely an agent of the law, the sainted guide toward "another purity," "some brighter period" of "sacred love" foreshadowed by her agon (344–45). What had been half-truth, half-delusion is rendered whole as a vision of progress through due process. And the bond she thus forges anew with the community lends another moral interpretation to her "new birth" as American. It recasts her adopted "forest-land" into the site of prophecy, home-to-be of the "angel or apostle of the coming revelation"; it reconstitutes Hester herself, *as a marginal dissenter*, into an exemplum of historical continuity (344–45).

We accept all this as inevitable, as readers did from the start, because Hawthorne has prepared us for it. His strategies of ambiguity and irony *require* Hester's conversion to the letter. And since the magistrates themselves do not impose the A; since the community has long since come to regard Hester as an "angel or apostle" in her own right; since, moreover, we never learn the process of her conversion to the A (while her development through the novel tends in exactly the opposite direction); since, in short, neither author nor characters help us—we must meet the requirement ourselves.

"The scarlet letter had not done its office," and, when it has, its office depends on our interpretation—or, more precisely, on our capacities to respond to Hawthorne's directives for interpretation. The burden this imposes can be specified by contrast with Dimmesdale's metamorphosis, earlier in the story, from secret rebel into prophet of New Israel. Hawthorne details the state of despair in which the minister agrees to leave, elaborates the disordered fantasies that follow, and yet leaves it to us to explain Dimmesdale's recantation. In this case, however, the explanation emerges directly from character and plot. "The minister," Hawthorne writes, "had never gone through an experience calculated to lead him beyond the scope of generally received laws; although, in a single instance, he had so fearfully transgressed one of the most sacred of them. But this had been a sin of passion, not of principle, nor even purpose" (290). When, accordingly, Dimmesdale decides to leave with Hester, he does so only because he believes he is "irrevocably doomed" (291), and we infer upon his return that he has regained his faith after all—that he has made peace at last with the Puritan ambiguities of mercy and justice, good and evil, head and heart, which he had abandoned momentarily in the forest.

The reasons for Hester's reversal are far more complex. It takes the whole story to work them through. To begin with, there is the problem of form, since in her case (unlike Dimmesdale's) the reversal so conspicuously defies tradition. I refer to the genre of tragic love to which *The Scarlet Letter* belongs. Had Hester returned for love alone (the A for Arthur) or under the cloud of disaster abroad (the A for adversity), we could follow her reasoning readily enough. But Hawthorne asks us to consider the disparity between these familiar tragic endings and Hester's choice. The familiar endings, from *Antigone* and *Medea* through *Antony and Cleopatra* and *Tristan and Isolde*, are variations on the theme of love against the world. Hester's return merges love *and* the world. In this aspect (as in others) it offers a dramatic contrast with European novels of adultery, which narrative theorists have classified in terms either of subversion or of containment, as implying "a fatal break in the rigid system of bourgeois realism," or as "work-[ing] to subvert what [the novel] aims to celebrate," or else (because of the "nearly universal *failure* of the adulterous affair") as serving "closurally to reinstate social norms."[1] *Madame Bovary* and *Anna Karenina* can be said to fit any of these descriptions. *The Scarlet Letter* fits none. Hester neither reaffirms her adulterous affair nor disavows it; her actions neither undermine the social order nor celebrate it; and at the end she neither reinstates the old norms nor breaks with them. Instead, she projects her dream of love onto some "surer ground" in the future, when "the whole relation between man and woman" can be reestablished. In other words, her return deliberately breaks with tradition by its emphasis on the political implications of process as closure.

The political emphasis is appropriate for the same reason that it is problematic: Hawthorne's portrait of Hester is a study of the lover as social rebel. Not as antinomian or witch, as he explicitly tells us, and certainly not as adulteress—if anything Hester errs at the opposite extreme, by her utter repression of eros. This emphasis on the non- or even antierotic is also to highlight sexual transgression, of course, but wholly by contrast; and it is to reinforce the contrast that Hawthorne insinuates by his often-remarked parallels between Hester and "unnatural" Anne Hutchinson, mother of "monstrous misconceptions"[2] as well as imperious, "bitter-tempered" Mistress Hibbins (217). Hawthorne remarks, with a note of disgust, that Hester had lost her "womanly" qualities, had become almost manlike in her harshness of manner and feature:

> Even the attractiveness of her person had undergone a . . . sad transformation . . . [so that] there seemed to be no longer any thing in Hester's face for Love to dwell upon; nothing in Hester's form, though majestic and statue-like, that Passion could ever dream of clasping in its embrace; nothing in Hester's bosom, to make it ever

again the pillow of Affection. Some attribute had departed from her, the permanence of which had been essential to keep her a woman. (258–59)

Hester errs, then, not in her sexual transgression but in her "stern development" as an individualist of increasingly revolutionary commitment (259). At the novel's center is a subtle and devastating critique of radicalism that might be titled "The 'Martyrdom' of Hester Prynne." It leads from her bitter sense of herself as victim to her self-conscious manipulation of the townspeople, and it reveals an ego nourished by antagonism; self-protected from guilt by a refusal to look inward; using penance as a refuge from penitence; feeding on shame, self-pity, and hatred; and motivated by the conviction that society is the enemy of the self.

Let me recall the scene I began with, in the chapter midway through the novel. Seven years have passed and the townspeople have come to regard Hester with affection, admiration, even reverence. On her part, Hester has masked her pride as humility, has repeatedly reminded them, by gesture and look, of her "saint-*like*" suffering, and in general has played upon their guilt and generosity until "society was inclined to show its *former* victim a more benign countenance than she cared to be favored with, or, perchance, than she deserved" (187, 257; my emphasis). And like other hypocrites in Hawthorne's work, Hester pays a heavy price for success. "All the light and graceful foliage of her character had been withered up," he tells us, "leaving a bare and harsh outline, which might have been repulsive, had she possessed friends or companions to be repelled by it" (258). She has none because she wants none. The "links that united her to the rest of human kind had all been broken," save for "the iron link of mutual crime" (255). She considers Pearl, whom she loves, an instrument of "retribution" (273). Concerning those to whom she ministers—not only "her enemies" but also those for whom "the scarlet letter had the effect of a cross on a nun's bosom"—Hawthorne points out that Hester "forebore to pray for [them], lest, in spite of her forgiving aspirations, the words of the blessing should stubbornly twist themselves into a curse" (258, 191).

It is worth stressing the severity of Hawthorne's critique. After seven years Hester has become an avenging angel, a figure of penance unrepentant, a so-called Sister of Mercy who not only scorns those who call her so but who has developed contempt for all "human institutions," "whatever priests or legislators had established" (257, 290). Despairing, therefore, of any improvement short of tearing down "the whole system of society" and doubtful even of that "remedy," she turns her energies first against "the world's law" and then against her daughter and herself (260, 259). Her heart, Hawthorne tells us,

> had lost its regular and healthy throb, [and she] wandered without a clew in the dark labyrinth of mind; now turned aside by an insurmountable precipice; now starting back from a deep chasm. There was wild and ghastly scenery all around her, and a home and comfort nowhere. At times, a fearful doubt strove to possess her soul, whether it were not better to send Pearl at once to heaven, and go herself to such futurity as Eternal Justice should provide. (261)

Here is the allegorical landscape of misguided rebellion: a wild, self-vaunting independence leading by a ghastly logic of its own to the brink of murder and suicide. No wonder Hawthorne remarks at this point that "the scarlet letter had not done its office."

I do not mean by this to deny the obvious. Hester is a romantic heroine. She is endowed with all the attributes this term implies of natural dignity, generosity of instinct, and what Hawthorne calls "a woman's strength" (257). Although she persistently abuses or represses these qualities, nonetheless they remain potential in her—dormant but felt in her every thought and action—and Hawthorne clearly means them to move us all the more forcefully for the contrast. As he remarks after detailing her "sad transformation," "She who has once been a woman, and ceased to be so, might at any moment become a woman again, if there were only the magic touch to effect the transfiguration. We shall see whether Hester Prynne were ever afterwards so touched, and so transfigured" (260). While we wait to see, Hester persistently invites our pity and praise, and by and large she succeeds, as she did with the Puritans. But to take her point of view is to prevent the scarlet letter from doing its office. It leads us, as it did Hester, into conflict—compels us to choose between the reasons of the heart and the claims of institutions—and conflict is precisely what the letter is designed to eliminate.

Again, a distinction is called for. Conflict is also a form of process, of course, but one that assumes inherent antagonism; it derives from a partiality that inspires partisanship. Conflict forces us to take positions and thus issues in active oppositions: one certainty against another, one generation against the next, one class or gender against another. Process (for Hawthorne) is a form of partiality that accepts limitation, acknowledges its own incompleteness, and so tends toward tolerance, accommodation, pluralism, acquiescence, inaction.

The contrary tendency toward conflict is the dark side of Hawthorne's chiaroscuro portrait of Hester. Her black eyes and hair—always a danger signal in Hawthorne's (culture's) symbolic system—are complemented, so to speak, by his relentless critical commentary on her every misstep into independence. We feel it the moment she crosses the prison threshold to his gently mocking "*as if* by her own *free-will*" (162; my emphasis). We see it detailed in her radical speculations, when her mind wanders

> without rule or guidance, in a moral wilderness as vast, as intricate and shadowy, as the untamed forest. . . . Her intellect and heart had their home, as it were, in desert places, where she roamed as *freely* as the wild Indian in his woods. . . . Shame, Despair, Solitude! These had been her teachers,—stern and wild ones,—and they had made her strong, but taught her much amiss. (290; my emphasis)

This running gloss on the ways that the letter has not done its office reaches its nadir in her forest meeting with Dimmesdale. Amidst the fallen autumn leaves, Hester discards the A in a gesture of defiance for which (Hawthorne reminds us) her entire seven years had been the preparation. "The past is gone!" she exclaims. "With this symbol, I undo it all, and make it as it had never been!" (292). And the narrator adds, with characteristic irony (characteristic, among other things, in that the irony borders on moralism):

> O exquisite relief! She had not known the weight, until she felt the *freedom!* . . . All at once, *as with* a sudden smile of heaven, burst forth the sunshine.
>
> Such was the sympathy of Nature—that wild, heathen Nature of the forest never subjugated by human law, nor illumined by higher truth—with the bliss of these two spirits! (292–93; my emphasis)

The narrator's ironies are not Hawthorne's precisely, and the difference, as we shall see, allows for a significant leeway in interpretation. But even within this larger perspective the contrast in forms of process is unmistakable. The radicalization of Hester Prynne builds on the politics of either/or. Hawthorne's symbolic method requires the politics of both/and. To that end, in the forest scene, Pearl keeps Hester from disavowing the office of the A, as earlier she had kept her from becoming another antinomian Anne or Witch Hibbins. Indeed, it is worth digressing for a moment to point out how closely for these purposes Pearl is bound to the A—with what painstaking care this *almost* anarchic figure is molded into a force for integration. Hawthorne presents in Pearl a profound challenge to the boundaries of socialization,* but he also details her restrain-

*I take up this issue in the last chapter, but it may be noted here, as intrinsic to Hawthorne's mode of ambiguity, that Pearl, who forces Hester to restore the A, is among other things an incarnation of Emersonian whim (not to say Poesque perversity)—a figure of "infinite variety," "mutability," and "caprice," with "wild, desperate, defiant" proclivities; the very spirit of

ing role with a consistency that verges on the didactic. He sustains this technique through virtually all her dialogues, with their conspicuously emblematic messages. And he reinforces it with his every definition of Pearl: as "imp" of the "perverse" *and* "pearl of great price," as "demon offspring," "Red Rose," "elf-child," and "mother's child" (Hester's "blessing" and "retribution" all in one); as the image simultaneously of "untamed nature" and the "angel of judgment," and, at the climactic election-day ritual, as (successively) "sin-born child," "witch-baby," the quintessential outsider who engages with and so weaves together all sections of the diverse holiday crowd—"even as a bird of bright plumage illuminates a whole tree of dusky foliage"—and, finally, as the fully "human" daughter who breaks once and for all the "spell" of mutual isolation (208, 211, 210, 215, 202–3, 205, 329, 330, 336, 339). Throughout this

---

negation, toward her inwardly rebellious mother no less than toward the apparent consensus of Puritan Boston (269–74)—and that all these traits, including the most "freakish" ("fiend-like," "demon offspring"), give symbolic substance to the "imperious gesture" with which Pearl asserts her "authority" in the forest scene (298–99):

> Pearl still pointed with her forefinger; and a frown gathered on her brow; the more impressive from the childish . . . aspect of the features that conveyed it. . . .
>
> "Hasten Pearl; or I shall be angry with thee!" cried Hester Prynne. . . .
>
> But Pearl, not a whit startled at her mother's threats, any more than mollified by her entreaties, now suddenly burst into a fit of passion, gesticulating violently, and throwing her small figure into the most extravagant contortions. . . . Seen in the brook, once more, was the shadowy wrath of Pearl's image, crowned and girdled with flowers, but stamping its foot, wildly gesticulating, and, in the midst of it all, still pointing its small forefinger at Hester's bosom! . . . .
>
> "Come thou and take it up!" (298–300)

Pearl's reflection in the brook is a memorable representation of the reciprocities of process and telos. It stands for nature (and the natural) as an office of repression. Equally and *simultaneously*, it stands for the demands of social conformity, indifferent to threat and entreaty, and conveyed through an impassioned willfulness. It is the letter of the law conceived in the spirit of resistant individuality, and vice versa.

development—in effect, our developing sense of Pearl as "the scarlet letter endowed with life"—Pearl serves increasingly to underscore what is wrong with Hester's radicalism, what remains "womanly" about Hester despite her manlike "freedom of speculation," and what sort of politics Hester must adopt if she is to help effect the changes that history calls for (204, 210, 259).

No other character in the novel, not even the shadowy Roger Chillingworth, is more carefully orchestrated into the narrative design or more single-mindedly rendered a means of orchestration. Midway through the story, at the midnight scaffold, Hawthorne pointedly presents us with a *figura* of things to come: "There stood the minister, with his hand over his heart; and Hester Prynne, with the embroidered letter glimmering on her bosom; and little Pearl, herself a symbol, and the connecting link between these two" (251). At the last scaffold scene Pearl kisses the minister, now openly her father at last, and Hawthorne remarks: "Towards her mother, too, Pearl's errand as a messenger of anguish was all fulfilled" (339). And with that office accomplished—by the one character, it will bear repeating, who might be imagined to offer an alternative vision in the novel—Hester can choose in due time to become the agent of her own domestication.

There is a certain irony here, to be sure, but it functions to support Hester's choice by reminding us of the burden of free will, when freedom is properly willed, for, although the burden is a tragic one, it alone carries the prospect of progressive (because incremental, nonconflictual) change. I discuss this use of irony in chapter 3. Let me say for the moment that it pertains above all to historical process and that it is perhaps especially prominent in Hawthorne's tales of the Puritans. The obvious contrast to Hester's return in this respect is the fate of Young Goodman Brown. Unlike Hester, Brown insists on alternatives when he rejoins the settlement—innocence or guilt, the truths of the town or those of the forest—and so finds himself in a hermeneutical impasse, a paralysis of thought and action whose issue is unambiguous "gloom." The no less obvious parallel (in view of Hester's propensities for the unillumined "sympathy of Nature") is the lovers' choice that ends "The May-Pole of Merry Mount." Strictly speaking, it is John Endicott, "the Puritan of Puritans," who forces the former "Lord and Lady of the May" into history. But in fact, Hawthorne emphasizes, they had started on that harsh, necessary road to progress long before, of their own free will: "From the moment they truly loved, they had subjected themselves to earth's doom of care, and sorrow, and troubled joy, and had no more a home at Merry Mount."[3]

Much the same might be said of Hester and Dimmesdale, although they must learn the lesson for themselves, separately, and offstage as it were—Dimmesdale, in the privacy of his study (following a "maze" of Goodman Brown–like temptations); Hester across the ocean, in the "merry old England" that the Puritans had rejected together with the Maypole (303, 211). Like Dimmesdale, she comes back home as a mixed figure of "pathos" and promise (333)—"angel of judgment" and mercy, "messenger of anguish" and hope. Hawthorne writes of the fully humanized Pearl, the former "wild child" who has at last "developed all her sympathies," that she would no longer need to "do battle with the world, but [could] be a woman in it" (339). It might be said of Hester upon her return that she can leave Pearl behind because she has taught herself to play Pearl to her own former Hester. She no longer needs restrictions because, after her long battle with the world, she has learned how to restrict herself—how to obviate the conflict between self and society, between the certainty of love and certain prospects of social change, between prophetic hope and politics as usual. As a woman in the world, she has learned to deflect, defuse, or at least defer that inherently explosive conflict and at best to transmute it, freely, into a faith that identifies continuity with progress.

This political level of meaning is closely connected to the moral. What I just called Hawthorne's politics of both/and is directly based upon his concept of truth. Critics often remark on the moral he draws from Dimmesdale's experience: "Be true! Be true! Be true!" (341). But, as usual with Hawthorne, it is hinged to the narrative by ambiguities. He tells us that he has culled the moral ("among many" others) from "a manuscript of old date," which he has "*chiefly* followed" (341; my italics). And he prefaces the moral with a dazzling variety of reports about the scarlet letter (or the absence of it) on the minister's breast. For Hawthorne, partiality is to process what multiplicity is to truth—a series of limited perspectives whose effectiveness depends on their being partial without becoming exclusive and partisan in such a way as gradually, by complementarity rather than conflict, to represent the whole. His political meaning here points us toward the premises of liberal society. His moral meaning is grounded in the premises of Puritan thought. The connection between the two is that between the Hobbist and the Calvinist meanings of the Fall. *The Scarlet Letter* is a story of concealment and revelation, where the point of revelation is not to know the truth but to embrace many truths and where concealment is not a crime, but a sin.

Not crime, but sin: Hawthorne adopts this fine theological distinction for his own liberal purposes. A crime pertains to externals, and, as a rule, it involves others, as in the case of murder or adultery. A sin pertains to the spiritual and internal, to an act of will. It may or may not involve crime, just as a crime (murder, for example, or adultery) *may* not involve sin. It depends on the inner cause, the motive. The issue, that is, is guilt, not shame: not the deceiving of others, but the skewing of one's own point of view. The political office of the A is to make partisanship an agent of reciprocity. Its moral office is to lead from the willful self-binding of a truth—paradigmatically, a truth of one's own—to the redemptive vision of many possible truths.

In the next-to-last chapter, that office is rendered (as the chapter title tells us) through "The Revelation of the Scarlet Letter" (332). The action centers on the scaffold, as it does twice previously. The first time is at Hester's midday "public exposure" (172), where the A denotes various kinds of division (within the community, within Dimmesdale, and, most dramatically, between Hester and the community). The second scaffold scene comes midway through the novel, in the midnight meeting that draws the main characters together, and by implication, the townspeople as well, for the A that flashes across the night sky lights up the entire town "with the distinctness of mid-day . . . [lending] another moral interpretation to the things of this world than they had ever borne before . . . as if [this] . . . were the light that is to reveal all secrets, and the daybreak that shall unite all who belong to one another" (251).

In short, the novel tends increasingly toward reconciliation through a series of ambiguous unveilings, each of which might be titled "The Revelation of the Scarlet Letter." In that penultimate chapter Dimmesdale reconciles himself with his guilt, with Pearl, with Hester, with Chillingworth, and, in "words of flame," with the destiny of New Israel (332). Now it only remains for Hester to join the telos in process. When she does so, in the conclusion, her moral interpretation of things past and future may be seen to reverse her first misstep across the prison threshold. Indeed, the scene deliberately echoes that initiation into concealment so as emphatically to invert it. When Hester returns, she pauses "on the threshold" of her old home—as many years before she had paused "on the threshold of the prison door"—long enough to display to the onlookers a scarlet letter on her breast (162, 343). It is a nice instance of liminality serving its proper conservative function at last. Then, at the start of her trials, Hester had repelled the beadle, representative of "the Puritanic code of law" (162), in order to assert "her own free-will." Now she returns as representative of the need for law and the limits of free will. Having abandoned the hope of erasing the past, Hester internalizes the past in all its shame and sorrow. Franz Kafka's penal colony requires a fatal mechanism of authority in order to make the prisoner accept his guilt; Hester preempts the mechanism by authorizing her own punishment and inscribing her guilt upon herself. In a gesture that both declares her independence *and* honors her superiors, she re-forms herself, voluntarily, as the vehicle of social order.

This moral design parallels the political process I outlined, but with an important difference. Hester's radicalism sets her apart and sustains her marginality to the end. The sin she commits (her double act of concealment, first of her lover, then of her husband) links her to everyone else. She is unique as a rebel but typical as a liar. Indeed, telling lies is the donnée of the novel as for the Puritans the prison is the donnée of their venture in utopia. It establishes the terms of human possibility in an adulterated world. Directly or indirectly—as deception, concealment, or hypocrisy, through silence (in Hester's case), cunning (in Chillingworth's), eloquence (in Dimmesdale's), or perversity (in Pearl's)—lies constitute the very texture of community in *The Scarlet Letter.* But the texture itself is not *simply* evil. All of Hawthorne's main characters are good people trapped by circumstance, all are helping others in spite of themselves, and all are doing harm for what might justifiably be considered the best of reasons: Hester for love, Dimmesdale for duty, and the Puritan magistrates for moral order. Even Chillingworth, that least ambiguous of villains, is essentially a good man who has been wronged, who lies in order to find the truth, who prods his victim to confess (partly, perhaps, through love), and who, in leaving his wealth to Pearl (gratuitously), provides the basis for whatever there is of a happy ending to the story.

Hawthorne owes this *complex* view of evil—good and evil entwined, the visible "power of blackness" symbiotically augmented by the pervasive if sometimes oblique power of light—to Puritan theology. As the New England primer put it, Adam's fall did much more than fell us all. It also brought the promise of grace through Christ, the Second Adam. Justice *and* mercy, law *and* love: from these twin perspectives, the Puritans built the scaffold and imposed the A. Restrictions were necessary because the Fall had sundered the affections from the intellect; it had set the truths of the heart at odds with the truths of the mind. Now only faith could reconcile the two kinds of truth. They who bound themselves to a single view, *either* justice *or* mercy, were entering into a Devil's pact. They were committing themselves to a lie by concealing a part of reality from themselves, including the reality of the self in all its ambiguity, both human and divine—hence, the degeneration of Chillingworth, "demon of the intellect" (321), and Dimmesdale, until he manages to harmonize the minister's gospel of love with the lover's self-punishment. Hence, too, Pearl's fragmented identity: she is a shifting collage of retribution and love, seeking integration; and, hence, the reciprocal movement of Hester and the community, from opposition to mutuality. As she acts the Sister of Mercy toward those who merely judged her, and so judged too harshly, Hester increasingly touches the people's "great and warm heart" (226). At the end, after she has passed judgment on herself, Hester gains a fuller, more generous vision of reality than she dreamed possible in the forest. Then it was love with a consecration of its own. Now her love has the consecration of justice, morality, and community.

I rehearse this familiar pattern in order to point out that nothing in it is random or arbitrary. Not a single aspect of this apparent multiplicity (reversals, revisions, and diverse points of view) permits free choice. Hawthorne's celebrated evasiveness comes with a stern imperative. Penitence, he would urge us, has more substance than the absolutism of either/or. Drab though it seems, the morality of both/and heightens personal vision by grounding it in the facts of experience. It takes more courage to compromise. It is a greater act of self-assertion to recognize our limits—to "be true" to what we most deeply are while admitting the fragmentary quality of our truth—to keep faith in our boldest convictions while acknowledging the incompleteness of those convictions, and so to discipline ourselves, of our "own free-will," to the pluralist forms of progress.

It amounts to a code of liberal heroics. Hawthorne's focus is first and last upon the individual; his emphasis on perspective assumes faith in ambiguity; and his ambiguities compel resolution through the higher laws of both/and. Through those higher laws we learn how to sustain certain ideals *and* deny the immediate claims of their certainty upon us; how to possess the self by being self-possessed (which is to say, to hold the self intact by holding it in check); and, from both of these perspectives, how voluntarily to embrace gradualism and consensus in the expectation that, gradually, "when the world should have grown ripe for it," consensus will yield proximate justice for the community and, for the individual, the prospect of unadulterated love.

The prospect leads from the moral to the aesthetic level of the novel. Again, Hawthorne himself provides the link—in this case through the parallel he assumes between moral bivalence and symbolic ambiguity. Consider the title he gives to that chapter midway through the novel. "Another View of Hester" means an inside view of her secret radicalism; it also means a public view of Hester through her acts of charity, which in turn involves a distinction between the view of the many, who consider her "angelic," and the view of the few, "the wise and learned men" who were reluctant to give up earlier "prejudices" (257). "Another view" means a true sight of Hester, as she really is (rather than as she appears), *and* it means a glimpse of Hester in medias res, in the process of development. Above all, it means another view in the sense of differences of interpretation: interpretation in the form of rumor and legend (the A that magically protects Hester "amid all peril"); interpretation as a mode of sacralization (the A as a nun's cross); interpretation as agent of social change; and interpretation as vehicle of manipulation (Hester "never raised her head to receive their greeting. If they were resolute to accost her, she laid her finger on the scarlet letter, and passed on. This might be pride, but was so like humility that it produced all the softening effects of the latter quality on the public mind"); and, of course, interpretation as the avenue to multiple meanings—the A as sign of infamy, pillow for the sick, shield against Indian arrows, "glittering" and "fantastic" work of art (257–58, 255).

All this and more. No critical term is more firmly associated with *The Scarlet Letter* than ambiguity. What has not been adequately remarked, and questioned, is the persistent, almost pedantic pointedness of Hawthorne's technique. F. O. Matthiessen defined Hawthorne's ambiguity as "the device of multiple-choice"[4]—and so it is, if we recognize it as a device for enclosure and control. That strategy can be traced on every page of the novel, from start to finish, in Hawthorne's innumerable directives for interpretation: from the wild rose he presents to his readers in chapter 1—in a virtuoso performance of multiple choice that is meant to preclude choice (for it instructs us *not* to choose between the local flower, the figural passion flower, and the legacy of the ambiguously "sainted Anne Hutchinson")—to the heraldic device with which the novel ends: the "engraved escutcheon" whose endlessly interpretable design (one "ever-glowing point of light gloomier than the shadow" but a source of relief nonetheless) "*might* serve for a motto *or* brief description of our now concluded tale" (345; my emphasis). Concluded *then*, but, by authorial direction, it is *now* in process, a prod to our continuing speculations. The "curious investigator may still discern [it]," Hawthorne remarks, "and perplex himself with the purport" (345), and the interplay between our perplexity and its purport, like that between process and telos in the description of the rose ("It *may* serve, let us hope, to symbolize *some* sweet moral blossom, that *may* be found along the track, *or* relieve the darkening close tale of human frailty and suffering"), tells us that meaning, while indefinite, is neither random nor arbitrary; rather, it is gradual, cumulative, and increasingly comprehensive (159; my emphasis).

The Scarlet Letter is an interpreter's guide into perplexity. As critics have long pointed out, virtually every scene in the novel is symbolic, virtually every symbol demands interpretation, and virtually every interpretation takes the form of a question that opens out into a variety of possible answers, none of them entirely wrong, and none in itself satisfactory. But the result (to repeat) is neither random nor arbitrary. It is a strategy of pluralism—issuing, on the reader's part, in a mystifying sense of multiplicity—through which each set of questions and answers is turned toward the same solution: all meanings are partly true, hence, interpreters must choose as many parts as possible of the truth and/or as many truths as they can possibly find in the symbol.

Let me illustrate my point through the single most straightforward instance of choice in the novel. Describing Hester's "sad transformation" (midway through the story), Hawthorne remarks that her "rich and luxuriant hair had either been cut off, or was . . . completely hidden by the cap" (259). For once, it seems, we have a plain truth to discover. Something has been hidden, a question about it has been raised, and we await the moment of disclosure; that moment reveals, of course, in "a flood of sunshine" (292), that Hester had *not* cut off her hair. But of course, too, Hawthorne means for us to recognize that in some sense she *had*—had cut off her "essential womanhood," had cut herself off from community, and had cut away her natural luxuriance of character by willfully hiding it beneath an Odysseus' cloak of conformity. These are metaphors, not facts. But in Hawthorne's ambiguous world a main function of choice is to blur the commonsense lines between metaphor and fact, and nowhere is that blurring process better demonstrated than at the moment of revelation, during her forest meeting with Dimmesdale, when Hester discards the A:

> By another impulse, she took off the formal cap that confined her hair; and down it fell upon her shoulders, dark and rich, with at once a shadow and a light in its abundance, and imparting the charm of softness to her features. There played around her mouth, and beamed out of her eyes, a radiant and tender smile, that *seemed* gushing from the very heart of womanhood. . . . Her sex, her youth, and the whole richness of her beauty, came back from *what men call* the irrevocable past. (292–93; my emphasis)

Shadow and light, seemed and was, irrevocable and renewed, womanhood cut off/hidden/lost/restored: *The Scarlet Letter* is a novel of endless points of view that together conspire to deprive us of choice. We are enticed by questions so that we can be allowed to see the polarity between seeking *the* answer, any answer, and undertaking an interpretation. The option is never one thing or another; it is all or nothing. We are offered an alternative, not between different meanings, but between meaning or meaninglessness, and it is meaning in that processual, pluralistic, and therefore (we are asked to believe) progressivist sense that Hester opts for when she returns to New England.

In that option lies the moral-aesthetic significance of Hawthorne's representation of crime as sin. Crime involves social transgression, as in the tradition of the detective story, which centers on the discovery of the criminal. Or, more equivocally, it might involve a conflict of rights that must be decided one way or another, as in the tradition of the novel of adultery, which opposes the claims of the heart to those of civic order. Hawthorne makes use of both kinds of plot, only to absorb them—climactically, through Hester's return—into a story about the trials and triumphs of ambiguity. Through the office of the scarlet letter, all particulars of the criminal act, together with the conflicts they entail, dissolve into a widening series of reciprocities. We come to see that the issue is not a breach of commandment, but (as Hawthorne signals by the conspicuous absence from the novel of the word "adultery") an incremental process of interpretation by which we discern the purport of the broken law for ourselves, and we do so by turning speculation against the tendency either to take sides or to view conflicting sides as irreconcilable.

To represent crime as sin is first of all to universalize the legal problem. It forces us to read a particular transgression in terms of innate human defects and the recurrent conflict of good and evil. But more comprehensively it makes the universal itself a curious object of interpretation—not in order to demystify it, not even to analyze it (in any cognitive sense), but, on the contrary, to invest it with richer significance and a more compelling universality. The ambiguities of *The Scarlet Letter* lead us systematically forward, from the political to the moral or religious to the aesthetic levels, toward what we are meant to understand is a series of broader and ampler meanings. *Always* ampler, and therefore at any given point indefinite: a spiral of ambiguities whose tendency to expand in scope and depth is all the more decisive for the fact that the process occurs in unexpected ways. The result is a liberal hierarchy of meaning, a series of unfoldings from simple to complex, "superficial" to "profound," which is as schematic, comprehensive, and coercive as the medieval fourfold system. Hawthorne's representation of crime as sin requires us to remain vague about all issues of good versus evil (except the evils of partiality and partisanship) in order to teach us that the Puritans' final, relatively nonconflictual view of Hester is deeper than the single-minded judgment reflected in the governor's iron breastplate, just as her final, relatively nonconflictual position toward their bigotry opens the way for both personal and historical development.

I have been using the term "option" in connection with Hester's return in order to stress the overriding distinction in Hawthorne's "device of multiple-choice" between making choices and having choice. His point is not that Hester finally makes a choice against adultery. It is that she has no choice but to resume the A. To make choices involves alternatives; it requires us to reject or exclude on the ground that certain meanings are wrong or incompatible or mutually contradictory. To have choice (in Hawthorne's fiction) is to keep open the prospects for interpretation on the grounds that reality never means either one thing or another but, rather, is Meaning fragmented by plural points of view, for, although the fragmentation is a source of many a "tale of frailty and sorrow," such as *The Scarlet Letter*, it is also, as *The Scarlet Letter* demonstrates, the source of an enriched sense of unity, provided we attend to the principles of liberal exegesis. And by these principles, to opt for meaning in all its multifariousness—to have your adulterous love and do the work of society too—is to obviate not only the conflicts embodied in opposing views but also the contradictions implicit in the very act of personal interpretation between the fact of multiple meaning and the imperative of self-assertion.

In other words, to interpret is willfully, in the interests of some larger truth, *not to choose*. Ambiguity is a function of prescriptiveness. To entertain plural possibilities is to eliminate possible divisions. We are forced to find meaning in the letter, but we cannot choose one meaning out of many: Chillingworth's fate cautions us against that self-destructive act of exclusion. Nor can we choose to interpret any of the novel's uncertainties as contradictions: the antagonism between Hester and the townspeople (or between Chillingworth and Dimmesdale, or between the minister and his conscience) cautions us repeatedly against that abuse of free will. What remains, then, is the alternative that symbols are lies, multiple choice is a mask for absence of meaning, and the letter is an arbitrary sign of transient social structures. And Hester's incipient nihilism cautions us at every turn against that flight from responsibility: in the first scene, by her instinctive attempt to conceal the letter; then, three years later, by concealing its meaning from Pearl (to Hawthorne's suggestion that "some new evil had crept into [her heart], or some old one had never been expelled"); later, in the forest scene, by flinging the letter "into infinite space" and drawing an (infinitely illusory) "hour's free breath"; and, finally, at the election day ritual, by gloating secretly at the prospect of its annihilation, a prospect that Hawthorne opens to her imagination so that, by absorbing it into what the entire novel makes us think *must* be some larger, truer interpretation, we can effectually exclude it as an alternative from our own (162, 274, 300).

If we refuse to exclude it—if we are tempted like Hester in the forest to reject meaning, if we make Chillingworth's choice at the scaffold against mercy or Dimmesdale's in his "secret closet" for contradiction (242)—then interpretation has not done its office. And lest, like these characters, we find ourselves wandering in a maze, Hawthorne points us toward the true path, midway in our journey through the novel. In "Another View of Hester" he impresses upon us: the need for personal interpretation; the inevitably partial nature of such interpretation; the richly varied experiential bases of interpretation; the tendency of these partial and shifting interpretations to polarize into symbolic oppositions, such as rumor and event, metaphor and fact, natural and supernatural, good and evil, head and heart, concealment and revelation, fusion and fragmentation; the need to recognize that these polarities, because symbolic, are never an inherent source of conflict, but instead they are always entwined in symbiotic antagonism and therefore mutually sustaining; and, as the key to it all, the *clavis symbolistica*, the need for faith both in the value of experience (shifting, private, and partial though it is) and in some ultimate hermeneutical complementarity, as in an ideal prospect that impels us toward an ever-larger truth.

That faith involves a *certain* activity on the reader's part. We need to make sense of the entire process for ourselves so that the process can in turn make sense of our partial contributions. The text elicits personal response in order to allow each of us to contribute to the expanding continuum of liberal reciprocity. It is a hermeneutics designed to make subjectivity the primary agency of change while keeping the subject under control, and it accomplishes this double function by representing interpretation as multiplicity flowing naturally into consensus. For, as oppositions interchange and fuse in the text, they yield a synthesis that is itself a symbol in process, an office not yet done. It is a richer symbol now than it was before, a higher office, but still veiled in the winding *perhaps*es, *or*s, and *might*s that simultaneously open new vistas of meaning and dictate the terms of closure.

It may be helpful to distinguish this strategy from others to which it has been compared. Hawthorne does not deconstruct the A; he does not anticipate the principle of indeterminacy; and he offers neither an aesthetics of relativism nor a dialectics of conflict. We might say that in some sense he is doing all of these things, but only in the sense that to do so is to dissipate the integral force of each. His purpose is to rechannel indeterminacy into pluralism, conflict into correspondence, and relativism into consensus. Insofar as terms such as "instability" and "self-reflexiveness" apply to *The Scarlet Letter*, they are agencies of a certain kind of interpretation, much as private enterprise and self-interest were said to be agencies of the general good in antebellum America. Frank Kermode's claim for Hawthorne's modernity—"his texts . . . are meant as invitations to co-production on the part of the reader"—is accurate in a sense quite different from that which he intended. Kermode speaks of "a virtually infinite set of questions." *The Scarlet Letter* holds out that mystifying prospect, much as Jacksonian liberals held out the prospect of infinite possibility, in order to implicate us as coproducers of meaning in a single, coherent moral-political-aesthetic design.[5]

This contrast pertains even more pointedly to Mikhail Bakhtin's concept of the dialogic imagination, which it has recently become fashionable to apply to American novels, and *The Scarlet Letter* in particular. Dialogics is the process by which a singular authorial vision unfolds as a "polyphony" of distinct voices. It entails a sustained open-ended tension between fundamentally conflicting outlooks. They are said to be conflicting insofar as they are *not* partial reflections (such as good or evil) of a more complex truth but each of them, rather, the expression of a separate and distinct way of understanding, a substantially different conception or configuration of good and evil. And they are said to be open-ended because the tension this involves is sustained *not* through the incremental layers of meaning but through the dynamics of diversity itself, which is, by definition, subversive of any culturally prescribed set of designs, including those of group pluralism. Bakhtin's dialogics denies telos through a "modernist" recognition of difference. Hawthorne's ambiguities imply telos through the evasion of conflict. They are modernist in the sense of modern middle-class culture—which is to say, in their *use* of difference (including marginality, complexity, and displacement) for purposes of social cohesion. Recent theorists such as Paul Ricoeur and Hans Blumenberg tell us that the novel (the genre par excellence of the dialogic) "legitimates the aesthetic qualities of *novitas*, . . . removes the dubiousness from what is new, and so *terra incognita*, or the *munda novus*, becomes possible."[6] Hawthorne seeks precisely to rein in what becomes possible. Aesthetically, it is the letter's office, as *novitas*, to enclose "the new world," whether as alternative order or as Bakhtinian carnival, within culture, *as* culture.

We might term this strategy the "monologics of liberal ambiguity." It serves to mystify hierarchy as multiplicity and diversity as harmony in process. Dialogics unsettles the link between process and closure. Hawthorne details the manifold discrepancies between process and closure in order to make discrepancy itself—incompleteness, concealment, the distance between penance and penitence—a vehicle of acculturation. To that end he guides his readers (as he does his errant heroine) to a *certain* belief in the unity of the symbol. He shows us that, precisely by insisting on difference, we can fuse an apparently (but not really) fragmented reality. Augustine's answer to Manichaean dualism was to redefine evil as the absence of good. Hawthorne's answer to the threat of multiplicity is to redefine conflict as the absence of ambiguity, and ambiguity, therefore, as the absence of conflict.

Ambiguity is the absence of conflict: Hawthorne's logic is as simple in theory as it is complicated in application. Historical facts tend toward fragmentation, but ambiguity brings this tendency under control, gives it purpose and direction, by ordering the facts into general polarities. Fragmentation itself thus becomes a function of consensus. For once the fragments have been ordered into polarities, the polarities can be multiplied ad infinitum, since each polarity entails or engenders other parallel, contrasting, or subsidiary sets of polarities. The process is one of endless variation upon a theme. And vice versa: it is a process of variation endlessly restricted to a single theme, because (in Hawthorne's fiction) all polarity is by definition ambiguous, all ambiguity is symbolic, and all symbols tend toward reconciliation—hence, the distinctly narrowing effect of Hawthorne's technique, in spite of his persistent allusions and deliberate elusiveness. He himself wrote of *The Scarlet Letter* to his publisher, James T. Fields, on November 3, 1850, that since the novel was "all in one tone" it could have gone on "interminably."[7] We might reverse this to say that what makes the novel hermeneutically interminable also makes it formally and thematically hermetic. In that sustained counterpoint between endlessness and monotone lies the dynamic behind Hawthorne's model of pluralist containment. Process for him is a means of converting the *threat* of multiplicity (fragmentation, irreconcilability, discontinuity) into the pleasures of multiple choice, where the implied answer, "all of the above," guarantees consensus.

The process of conversion follows the symbolic logic of the scarlet letter. It is the office of the A to demonstrate that naturally, organically, pluralism tends to absorb differences into polar opposites, and that bipolarity, properly interpreted, tends of its own accord toward integration. So conceived, the monologics of ambiguity in *The Scarlet Letter* extend to structures of gender, religion, history, psychology, aesthetics, morality, and epistemology. One instance, a minor one but suggestive of Hawthorne's range, is the imaginary "Papist" at the first scaffold scene (166), who sees Hester as the Virgin Mother and who seems to offer an option—an oppositional view, in Raymond Williams's sense, or, more accurately (in light of Hawthorne's emphasis on the relative newness in 1642 of the Reformation), a residual view—that goes deeper than personal and partial differences of perspective.[8] But here, as elsewhere, Hawthorne's point is to intrigue us with notions of conflict in order to disperse them. He can be said to have invented the Papist (that Puritan symbol of irreconcilable antagonism) on our behalf as an early step in our education in ambiguity, and the education proceeds through our recognition, in due time, that the putative contrast is really just one pole in the reciprocity between justice and love. Thus, Catholic and Protestant outlooks merge, midway through the novel, in the townspeople who interpret the A sympathetically as "a cross on a nun's bosom" and, more powerfully, at the final scaffold scene, in the apparent pietà, where Hester (in an image that prepares us for her final role as prophet) plays Sacred Mother to Dimmesdale's Christ (258, 339).

It makes for a rich fusion of polarities, with multiple implications for Hawthorne's symbolic method. For example, the papist perspective (if I may call it so) clearly parallels the compassionate view of Hester expressed by the young mother at the prison door, and clearly, Hawthorne presents *her* view mainly for purposes of contrast, as he does the Papist's, to highlight the harshness of Puritan judgment, whether from magistrates or from "matrons" (161). In each case the contrast turns out to be a form of symbolic doubling. The "young wife, holding a child by the hand," in some sense mirrors Hester; the embittered matrons in some sense preview Hester's later "injustice"—her impenitent, sometimes brutal judgments (variously motivated by "scorn," "hatred," and "asperity") of her perceived "enemies," her husband, and even her daughter (161, 269, 274). The result is a spiral of symbolic reciprocities, reinforced by principles of psychology (head-heart) and morality (good-evil), which grow increasingly comprehensive in their image of womanhood—increasingly comprehensive and, proportionately, increasingly positive. They find their high point in Hester the prophet: the rehumanized (because refeminized) heroine whose fall, though it warrants "strict and severe" censure (274), augments the promise she represents of future good things. The revelation is still to come, but Hester at last has reached the proper *womanly* vantage point for perceiving something of its import; she has earned the privilege of paying homage, if not directly to Hawthorne's "little Dove, Sophia," as several critics have argued, then to the dream of "sacred love," which Sophia shared with Nathaniel and which largely derived from the mid-nineteenth-century cult of domesticity (344).[9]

A similar strategy of incorporation applies to the parallel between the Papists and the other non-Puritan culture represented at the first scaffold scene. I refer to the local Indians, who judge from Hester's "brilliantly embroidered badge" that she "must needs be a personage of high dignity among her people" (330). Hawthorne invests the story's Indians with much the same processual-symbolic effect as he does the Catholic. He juxtaposes the outsider's perspective, in both cases, to that of the Puritans in order to absorb historical difference into what we are meant to think of as broader, universal categories. To that end he deploys the keywords of savagism: "stone-headed" implements, "snake-like" features, "savage finery," "painted barbarians," and, most frequently, "wild"—"wild Indian," "wild men . . . of the land," the "wildness" of their "native garb" (318, 329, 315, 330, 169).

It makes for an all-too-familiar Romantic-Jacksonian configuration: the primitive as an early stage of social growth, which the civilized state not only supersedes but (in the process) ingests, so that at its best society combines the "natural" state with the "higher" advantages of culture. Hence, the Indian aspect of Pearl, the "wild child" (329), and, above all, the Indian wildness of Hester's radicalization:

> Her intellect and heart had their home, as it were, in desert places, where she roamed as freely as the wild Indian in his woods . . . criticizing all with hardly more reverence than the Indian would feel for the clerical band, the judicial robe, the pillory, the gallows, the fireside, or the church. (290)

An entire culture is represented in these cunningly compressed polarities. Hawthorne appreciates the natural freedom of the "red men" (287), just as he deplores the civilized excesses of the Puritan pillory—and vice versa; he recognizes the dangers of "desert places" just as he acknowledges the need for fireside and church. It is an ambiguity that effectually deprives the Indians of both nature and civilization, a high literary variation on an imperial rhetoric that ranges from Francis Parkman's elegies for a "noble," "primitive," "dying" race to what Herman Melville satirized as "the metaphysics of Indian-hating."[10] Here it serves to empty the "savages" of their own history so as to universalize them as metaphors for Hester's development.

As all of these examples suggest, the basic symbolic opposition in *The Scarlet Letter* is that between self and society. I said earlier that Hawthorne portrays Hester as an individualist of increasingly radical commitment. I might as well have said a radical of increasingly individualist commitment, for Hawthorne's aim is to counter the dangerously diverse social possibilities to which she has access, in fantasy or fact—Indian society, witch covens, Elizabethan hierarchy, Leveler and Ranter utopia (289, 313–30)—to bring all such unruly alternatives under control, rhetorically and hence morally and politically, by implicating them all under the symbol of the unrestrained self.

No symbol was better calculated to rechannel dissent into the gradualism of process. And no symbol was more deeply rooted in the culture. As *The Scarlet Letter* reminds us, it served as a major Puritan strategy of socialization, through a process of inversion that typifies all such strategies. Society in this polar opposition became the symbol of unity, and the unsocialized self was designated the symbol of chaos unleashed—"sin, in all its branches," as the Reverend John Wilson details them in the first scaffold scene for "the poor culprit's" sake (176). Or, mutatis mutandis, the unsocialized self was a morass of "monstrous misconceptions," as John Winthrop labeled Anne Hutchinson, and society stood not just for legal order (as against antinomianism), but for Order at large—"the laws of nature and the laws of grace" (to quote Winthrop again) through which "we are bound together as one man."[11]

In either case, the polarity of self and society remained central through the successive discourses of libertarianism, federalism, republicanism, and Jacksonian individualism. Its negative pressures, implicit in Hawthorne's reference to "the sainted Anne Hutchinson" (and explicit in his essay on "Mrs. Hutchinson")—as well as in recurrent charges of antinomianism against those who were said to have "sprung up under her footsteps" (159), from Edwards through Emerson—are memorably conveyed in Alexis de Tocqueville's contrast between "traditional" and "modern" modes of control: "The ruler no longer says: 'You must think as I do or die.' He says: 'You are free to think differently, and to retain your life, your property, and all that you possess; but from this day on you are a stranger among us.'" Its positive form can be inferred from Edwin Chapin's Massachusetts election day sermon of 1844, *The Relation of the Individual to the Republic.* The self, Chapin argues, denotes "matters of *principle*" and society entails "matters of *compromise*," but in the American way of "self-government" (as nowhere else) it is "compromise not *of* principle but *for* principle."[12]

The Scarlet Letter is the story of a stranger who rejoins the community by compromising for principle, and her resolution has far-reaching implications about the symbolic structures of the American ideology. First, the only plausible modes of American dissent are those that center on the self: as stranger or prophet, rebel or revolutionary, lawbreaker or Truth seeker, or any other adversarial or oppositional form of individualism. Second, whatever good we imagine must emerge—and, properly understood, *has* emerged and is continuing to emerge—from things as they are, insofar as these are conducive to independence, progress, and other norms of group pluralism. And third, radicalism has a place in society, after all, as the example of Hester demonstrates—radicalism, that is, in the American grain, defined through the ambiguities of both/and, consecrated by the tropes of theology ("heaven's time," "justice and mercy," "divine providence"), and interpreted through the polar unities at the heart of American liberalism: fusion and fragmentation, diversity as consensus, process through closure.

Chapter Two

The Ironies of A-History

IN THE SPIRIT OF INTEGRATION Hester comes home to Puritan New England. Or rather, she comes home to the Puritan New England of antebellum America. For, of course, Hawthorne's immigrant community, like the letter it imposes, is a cultural artifact—a very sophisticated one, to be sure, and brilliantly embroidered with his personal concerns and intricate ambiguities, but woven nonetheless out of the same cultural cloth that by 1850 had produced the myth of the Puritan origins of the American Way. Hawthorne's return to roots involves far more than a private genealogy. For all their flaws, his Hathorne forebears were part of a venture that he believed marked the first stage of American nationhood. It is no accident that Dimmesdale's sermon on the future celebrates the transition of government from John Winthrop to John Endicott. The unspoken link between these two governors is nothing less than the nationalist tradition that connects Hester to Hawthorne. It represents the unfolding process of American self-determination, from Winthrop, the Ur-father, through Endicott, the Ur-patriot, whose rending of "the Red Cross from New England's banner" (Hawthorne writes elsewhere) was "the first omen of that deliverance which our fathers consummated" in 1776.[1]

These mythic Puritans have had a long, rich, and varied life in American historiography. By mid-century they had provided a native heroic age to displace Old World tradition; a common point of reference for a loose collection of regional "peoples"; a model of acculturation for a diversity of immigrant groups; a sacred mission to mask the motives of imperialism; a language of prophecy (antedating nationhood) through which the separation from England was declared a fulfillment of promise as well as a new beginning; an indigenous national past through which the (civil) war of independence was recast as a united struggle against foreign tyranny; and a cultural meta-identity ("utopians," "visionaries," "freedom-seekers," "pilgrims") within which to meld and remold the raw facts of credal, social, and ethnic difference.

As Hawthorne incorporates these various themes, they open into a crucial contrast between Puritanism in Old and New England. The contrast itself, like most other aspects of Hawthorne's view of the Puritans, was cultural commonplace. According to general belief at mid-century—one that was shared, among others, by New York's cultural pundit, Evert Duyckinck (a founder of the Young America movement and Hawthorne's major advocate in the literary world), the country's leading poet, Henry Wadsworth Longfellow (Hawthorne's lifelong friend and his first important reviewer), the epic historian of the era, George Bancroft (who helped Hawthorne secure his appointment as surveyor at the Salem Customs House), and the Manifest Destinarian John Louis O'Sullivan (Hawthorne's main publisher in the 1840s and godfather to his first child, Una)—there were two Puritan revolutions in the early 1600s. One was the Puritan exodus to the New World. It was a revolution for liberty that offered a model of progress by harnessing the energies of radicalism to the process of settlement, consolidation, and expansion. The Old World counterpart was the Puritan revolution (1642–49) that failed. Hawthorne suggests the reason for failure in his essay on Oliver Cromwell, which relates a "strange accident" in Cromwell's infancy when a huge ape, which was kept in the family, snatched up little Noll [as Oliver was nicknamed] in his fore-paws and clambered with him to the roof of the house. . . . The event was afterwards considered an omen that Noll would reach a very elevated station in the world."[2] It is a parable for the embittered young radical whose clambering "enthusiasm of thought" (260) Hawthorne details in that multifaceted midway chapter, "Another View of Hester":

> [This] was an age in which the human intellect, newly emancipated, had taken a more active and wider range than for many centuries before. Men of the sword had overthrown nobles and kings. Men bolder than these had overthrown and rearranged—not actually, but within the sphere of theory, which was their most real abode—the whole system of ancient prejudice, wherewith was linked much of ancient principle. Hester Prynne imbibed this spirit. She assumed a freedom of speculation, then common enough on the other side of the Atlantic, but which our forefathers, had they known of it, would have held to be a deadlier crime than that stigmatised by the scarlet letter. In her lonesome cottage by the sea-shore, thoughts visited her, such as dared to enter no other dwelling in New England; shadowy quests . . . perilous as demons. (259)

The controlling image is "forefathers." It carries the entire force of the ideological contrast I outlined: on one hand, the English Puritan revolution and all it prefigured, including what Hawthorne calls "the terrorists of France" (165); on the other hand, the Puritans who preserved "ancient principle" (along with "ancient prejudice") and whose broad reforms, therefore, sired the New World process that eventuated in national independence. This symbolic polarity, in which the Old World figures as social, moral, and spiritual antagonist, pervades Jacksonian writing. Its structure is generational and patriarchal, a tripartite renunciation of Europe, ascending from immigrant forefathers to fathers of independence to revolutionary sons, the latter being (at any given moment, in any period) always a generation in transition, on probation, committed to both filiopietism and progress. Invariably, that balancing act is a reenactment of the New World exodus: in some form, a recapitulation of the flight from an oppressive Old World, followed by a rededication to the (continuing) conquest of the American Canaan.

In the Jacksonian period the terms of flight pivoted on a contrast of Puritanisms; its object was the apotheosis of the American Revolution and constitutional democracy. As Ralph Waldo Emerson put it, John Winthrop and George Washington were agents of "futurity," whereas Oliver Cromwell and Napoleon Bonaparte substituted one form of tyranny for another:

> There is a sort of great ruffians that appear in such crises in human society to profit by a timely boldness & intrude themselves in the hour of peril into places, that are in quiet times above their capacity & fortunc. . . . Bear witness England & France in their Regicide Revolutions. Nameless & birthless scoundrels climbed up in the dark [like little Noll upon the ape], & sat in the sects of the Stuarts & Bourbons. Cromwell & Napoleon plucked them down when the light returned & locked their own yoke round the necks of mankind.

This was the broad view of thc transatlantic contrast; its particular application to Puritanism in Old and New England is summarized in a New Year's editorial, "America in 1846," in the widely influential *United States Magazine and Democratic Review*:

> [While] Cromwell, raised to power and to lofty fame . . . was degrading his great trust into the state offices of a military despot . . . [while] in the Old World, the dark spirit of bygone ages could not be exorcised . . . [there appeared a group of Puritans] who, full of devotion and of faith in their glorious mission, sought in the New World the only true spot whereon to build institutions which were to spring from and protect the real welfare and freedom of man.[3]

The contrast marked something of a conservative revision of Puritan roots. An earlier generation had looked back to Cromwell (along with Winthrop) as a precedent for the colonists' struggle against royal tyranny; the Jacksonians reversed that judgment to accommodate the needs of a different age.* On this issue, as on all others relating to the national past, the authoritative statement for the period is Bancroft's *History of the United States.* It describes Cromwell as a courageous man who for a time espoused the popular cause but, lacking "the principles of Puritan reforms," rapidly degenerated into a "despot"; devoid of any "love for ideal excellence, he abhorred the designs and disbelieved the promises of democracy. . . . There could be no republic" under him. At this same time, Bancroft continues, the Puritans in New England began the journey toward the liberal state. Our forefathers represented "not the Christian clergy, but the Christian people, the interpreter of the divine will; and the issue of Puritanism was popular sovereignty . . . a government in America such as the laws of natural justice warranted." Hence the divergent traditions of revolution in the modern world:

> For Europe there remained the sad necessity of revolution. . . . There was no relief for the nations but through revolution, and their masters had poisoned the weapons which revolution must use.

*Historians and orators of the revolutionary period and early republic are generally favorable toward Cromwell—conspicuously so, by contrast with the English tradition, from Edward Clarendon's royalist *History of the Rebellion* through Denzil Holles's "Memoirs" (1699) to David Hume's 1778 *History of England.* The "founding" generation of Americans praised Cromwell as the harbinger of a democratic order; the next generation used him as the exemplum of the wrong kind of revolution. By the end of the nineteenth century the assessment had reverted to admiration, as in the plays of Thomas Nield and George Townsend, the fiction of John M. Dean, and the various biographies listed in Frederic Harrison's *George Washington and Other American Addresses* (New York: Macmillan, 1901). The shifting views of Cromwell suggest that Bancroft's polarization is part of a larger cultural symbolic complementarity. This is in fact manifest in the figure of the immigrant regicide, such as Hawthorne's Gray Champion, who not only combines the good and bad aspects of Puritanism but also represents the link between Old and New World Puritans. It is a pervasive image in the literature of the time, from James McHenry's *The Spectre of the Forest* (1823) and the anonymous *Witch of New England* (1824) through James Fenimore Cooper's *The Wept of Wish-Ton-Wish* (1829) and Delia Bacon's *The Regicides* (1831) to Henry William Herbert's *Ruth Whalley; or The Fair Puritan* (1844).

> In America [however] a new people had risen up. . . . more sincerely religious, better educated, of serener minds, and of purer morals than the men of any former republic. . . . Democratic liberty and independent Christian worship at once existed in America . . . [and from the start they were the twin agents] of peaceful amelioration, gradual improvement, and spreading enlightenment. . . . The New England immigrants were the servants of posterity . . . the men who, as they first trod the soil of the New World, scattered the seminal principles of republican freedom and national independence. . . . [Thus] America developed her choice from within herself. . . . A revolution, unexpected in the moment of its coming, but prepared by glorious forerunners, grew naturally and necessarily out of the series of past events. . . . [When the] hour of the American revolution was come . . . [the] people of the continent . . . obeyed one general impulse, as the earth in spring listens to the command of nature.[4]

"America developed her choice from within herself": the revisionist contrast between Cromwell's revolt and the Great Migration effectually completed the rhetorical separation, long underway, of the New World from the Old. The revolutionaries had used the metaphor of coming-of-age as a rationale for independence; the Jacksonians extend their meaning back to origins: to an act of auto-conceptualization ("seminal principles" of, by, and for a New World) that issued "at once" in "a new people." And with that declaration of *cultural* independence came a sweeping distinction in the very meaning of revolution. In the Old World revolution meant recurrent violence; in the New, it meant "peaceful amelioration" and "spreading enlightenment," a process as organic and rejuvenating as seasonal rebirth, when "the earth in spring listens to the command of nature."

That was essentially Hawthorne's outlook as well. He sought to deepen, complicate, and refine it, and in doing so he often ridiculed its self-serving rhetoric and naive flights of optimism—he even may be said to have deconstructed its excesses of chauvinism—but it was never his intention to defy or subvert. Bancroft articulated the theory of American progress in all its crude emergent power. Within that cultural symbology, the ironic development from theocracy to democracy is a persistent theme in Hawthorne's fiction: in his children's writings and historical sketches, many of his best stories, and all of his novels—most explicitly in his second romance, *The House of the Seven Gables* (1851), in which the socialization of Hester Prynne is replayed in a "sunny" mood as the deradicalization of the artist Holgrave (a man with "a law of his own," converted to liberal domesticity); most intricately in his last completed novel, *The Marble Faun* (1860), which traces the transformations of humanity from paganism through Catholicism to Protestant America (the final stage, capped by Hilda's return to the "sunlight on [New England's] mountain tops");[5] and most subtly and fully in *The Scarlet Letter.* So considered, the novel's introduction registers a double genesis: the customshouse is entry at once to national history and to the history of the symbol. And in either sense the meaning of history centers on the significance of the Great Migration, a venture in "Utopia" (Hawthorne suggests at the start of the novel) that bases its dreams of "human virtue and happiness"—its sense of "special mission" and hope of a "daybreak that shall unite all who belong to one another"—on a true sight of sin (158, 332–33, 251).

Irony is the key to the historical contrasts and continuities involved. Critics have elaborated upon Hawthorne's ironic sense of history from what would seem to be every possible angle, except that of historical context. We have heard much about the moral depth, psychological insight, vast learning, and exquisite indirection of Hawthorne's representation of the past.* It may be added without in any way diminishing such

*What distinguishes these critical readings from mine is their insistence on Hawthorne's "detachment." This is the basis even for the historicist approach that characterizes the brilliant succession of scholars from Roy Harvey Pearce and David Levin through Michael D. Bell, culminating in Michael J. Colacurcio's *The Province of Piety: Moral History in Hawthorne's Early Tales* claims that his ironic mode is an expression of its time and place. Like his mode of ambiguity, it is grounded in liberal thought. Indeed, the two modes may be described as complementary poles of Hawthorne's aesthetics of liberalism. His ambiguities function as directives to narrative unity: they teach us to synchronize different layers of history by gathering a diversity of meanings within a single, self-enclosed symbol. His ironies are directives to the interpretation of chronology: they teach us to differentiate within the narrative between levels of historical development. I refer to the liberal concept of development: oblique, gradualistic, and cumulative. To see the past ironically is to affirm a design working itself out in such a way that, in Hawthorne's famous adage, "Man's accidents are God's purposes." As the eminent antebellum historian John Lothrop Motley put it, the point was "to discover a law out of all this apparently chaotic whirl and bustle. . . . That law is progress—slow, confused, contradictory, but ceaseless develop-

(Cambridge, Mass.: Harvard University Press, 1984). In the most balanced overview to date of the scholarship, George Dekker concludes that Hawthorne was a "writer too detached from any public 'place,' creed, or leader ever to commit himself unreservedly" (*The American Historical Romance* [Cambridge: Cambridge University Press, 1987], 130). Dekker sets this view persuasively within the framework of "Romantic irony." I would suggest that it also reflects a cultural presupposition that Hawthorne shares with his critics, then and now—namely, that not "to commit [oneself] unreservedly" is to commit oneself with reservations to many different meanings of "place, creed, or leader," and so to gain a larger synchronic perspective on them all. Some such presupposition may underlie as well Colacurcio's concept of the "plausible" and the "admirable" in his monumental explication of Hawthorne's "deconstructive" ironies: "This is how we always decide the question of irony: how plausible—and how admirable—is the literary result?" (*Province of Piety*, p. 209). In any case, the image of a detached Hawthorne runs counter to biographical facts, except for the biographical fact of his careful authorial self-construction, both officially—as in his contribution to Richard Henry Stoddard's biographical essay of 1853—and privately, in conversation and correspondence (e.g., *The Letters, 1843–1853* of the Centenary Edition, ed. Thomas Woodson, L. Neal Smith, and Norman Holmes Pearson [Columbus, Ohio: Ohio State University Press, 1985], 12: 277–78, 340).

ment, intellectual and moral"—for, as he wrote to Oliver Wendell Holmes, it is "a law of Providence that progress should be by spiral movement, so that when we seem most tortuous we may perhaps be going [most rapidly] ahead."[6]

The ironic model was the story of the Fall, in which a tortuous act of disobedience issues in the promise of a greater Eden. Its central example in sacred history was the agon of Christ. The prime example in what Motley called (in his letter to Holmes) "the rapidly developing history of our country" was the Janus-faced retro-progressive legacy of Puritan New England. Considered narrowly, in their own terms, the Puritans (as represented throughout the literature) were encumbered by "the prejudices of the past"; "they were strangely confused," addicted to "many errors," "nourished with . . . sometimes a mistaken zeal," and in many ways "as intolerant and narrow-minded as [any] bigots of . . . a remoter age." Thus "the superficial observer" may "sneer" at "the sect itself," but in the long view "Puritanism . . . was Religion struggling in, with, and for the People; a war against tyranny and superstition." "'Its absurdities . . . were the shelter for the noble principles of liberty.' . . . It was its office to engraft the new institutions of popular energy":

> [A] shallow philosophy . . . judges sects or parties, by the single acts or declarations of individuals, whose errors are often the fault of the age, or the temperament of the man, or the mere excess of reaction, rather than by their fundamental principles, which, lying at the base of the system, must in the end make themselves felt and acknowledged, and thenceforth characterize the action of their adherents. . . . The apparent results of the promulgation of great truths are often for a time equivocal, and even paradoxical. The weight at the end of a cord passing over a pulley follows the hand that draws it, though moving in a contrary direction. The true results are slowly developed.[7]

"Slowly," "contrary direction," "equivocal, and even paradoxical," "apparent results" to be interpreted either by the partial judgments of "shallow philosophy" or by the "fundamental principles" of incremental truth: in these terms Jacksonian spokesmen outlined "THE PURITAN SCHEME OF NATIONAL GROWTH." Through that scheme—blending (from the past) the "mysteries" of providential history with the "spiral movement" of sacred history and (from the present) Whig gradualism with Romantic organicism—they proposed to "examine and estimate the work of our Fathers" in order to "animate ourselves . . . in attempting our own great office in the world."[8] Essentially, Hawthorne shared those assumptions. His ironies have little in common with the modern irony of the absurd (as in Samuel Beckett's godless *Waiting for Godot*), and they are equally distant from the ironies of either Greek fate or German dialectics. Sophocles' *Oedipus* and Euripides' *Bacchae* assume a fatal divergence between human interests and the divine plan. G. W. F. Hegel and Karl Marx assume the prospect of an objective understanding that allows us to become conscious agents of Necessity. Hawthorne's irony denies fatalism and agency alike. It reveals a devious, unpredictable, often "tortuous," but eventually benevolent pattern, and invites us to recognize that our best recourse is to let it be.

We would not be wrong to see in this pattern the historiographical equivalent of laissez-faire. Its ironic premise, counterpart to Adam Smith's concept of the invisible hand, is the providential unconscious. The popular lyceum lecturer Richard Salter Storrs defined it in Whig terms as the "*indirect* relation" between means and ends: "while we recognize without flinching the fact that [the Puritans] erred, let us recognize also as clearly the fact that . . . [they were] preeminent among the men of their age . . . the real architects of Empire! Unconsciously they had struck here the vein whose quarried gold was to build and adorn the great fabrics of State throughout the future." Jared Sparks, the Jacksonian biographer laureate, and George Perkins Marsh, the prominent jurist and diplomat, chose the Romantic organic metaphor:

> it is sometimes a full century between seed time and harvest. A principle never produces its legitimate fruits, until it is precisely and distinctly enunciated, and men often act in partial accordance with truth, from some dim and half unconscious apprehension of its spirit, long before any master mind has clearly developed and proclaimed it.
>
> The more we look into the history of the colonies, the more clearly we shall see that the Revolution was not the work of a few years only, but began with the first [Puritan] settlement of the country; the seeds of liberty, when first planted here, were the seeds of the Revolution; they sprang forth by degrees; they came to maturity gradually; and when the great crisis took place, the whole nation were prepared to govern themselves, because unconsciously they always had in reality governed themselves.

Probably the fullest explanation comes in Horace Bushnell's influential oration of 1849, "The Fathers of New England," alternately titled "The Founders Great in Their Unconsciousness":

> The very greatness of these men . . . is that so little conceiving the future they had in them, they had a future so magnificent . . . a wisdom wiser than they knew, in principles more quickening and transforming than they could even imagine themselves. . . . [Thus it was that] our fathers had . . . little thought of a separation from the mother country. . . . And yet [they soon set out a "constitution," in their 1650 Body of Laws, which rendered them], . . . in fact, a little, independent, unconscious republic, unfolding itself . . . on its own basis, under its own laws; so that when the war of independence came . . . it stood ready in full form for action. . . .
>
> This was the . . . undesigning agency of the fathers of New England, considered as the authors of those great political and social issues which we now look upon as the highest and crowning distinctions of our history. Their ideal was not in these, but [they had] . . . a high constructive instinct, raising them above their age and above themselves; creating in them fountains of wisdom deeper than they consciously knew, and preparing in them powers of benefaction that were to be discovered only by degrees and slowly, to the coming ages.[9]

The providential unconscious allows for agency only by indirection and for understanding only through irony. Irony decodes the purpose behind the accident; it reveals the good we derive from evils past; it exposes the evils we do as we try to improve upon the past; and it demonstrates, "by degrees and slowly," that, evil and accident notwithstanding, improvement is the law of history.

"There is no instance, in all history," wrote Hawthorne in 1852,

> of the human will and intellect having perfected any great moral reform by methods which it adapted to that end; and the progress of the world, at every step, leaves some evil or wrong on the path behind it, which the wisest of mankind, of their own set purpose, could never have found the way to rectify.[10]

I quote this grim rebuke to radicals and reformers to show that, even at his most skeptical, Hawthorne assumes (as the a priori of interpretation) *standards* of wisdom, *visible signs* of the "progress of the world," and the *experience* of "great moral reform." His grand truth is Yes, in irony, and all the heaped-up folly of mankind cannot make him say No. For (in this view) those who say No, despair, having been misled by their "own purposes," whereas ironists see through the man-mocking balances of cultural loss and gain to the "powers of benefaction" of which evil itself is an "undesigning agency." Consider the progress of Christianity from the medieval Church through the Reformation. Consider the story of the United States in modern times; did not the Revolution, for all its savage excesses, mark a higher stage than the Great Migration? So, too, the Constitution, despite its omissions and suppressions, marked a higher stage than the *Mayflower* and *Arabella* compacts, republicanism (even in its Jacksonian form) a higher stage than Puritan theocracy, democracy (even in its theocratic form) than aristocracy, Protestantism (even in its Puritan form) a higher stage than Catholicism, Christianity (even in its Catholic form) a higher stage than paganism (whether of Merry Mount, Monte Beni, or "the wild Indian in his woods"), and American liberty (even in the Salem Customs House) a higher stage than European ideology, whether conservative, as in royal despots, or radical, as in French "terrorists" of 1793–94, 1830, and 1848–49.

It is a tribute to the imaginative richness of this outlook that virtually all these transformations are implicit in the novel's conclusion. From pagan forest and medieval "superstition" to Renaissance aristocracy (with its ornamental luxury and exotic "armorial seals"), and thence from the "succession" of customs-house appointees (royal-provincial, national-democratic) to the projected angel of the "coming revelation," they converge in a sort of imagistic dumb show of transition and ascent (340–44). That is the historical background to Hester's act of reconciliation. Hawthorne stresses that she resumes the A voluntarily in order to remind us one more time that *what is* is something from which society not only has evolved but will evolve. It is the climax of a long series of similar directives for interpretation, and Hawthorne dramatizes the irony it entails through the prophecies that precede and follow upon Hester's return. Dimmesdale's vision of the future emerges from the Puritans' view of themselves; it comes to us, accordingly, through reports of others, and it expresses "what each [listener] knew better than he could hear or tell" (332). By contrast, Hester's vision lies so far into the future that others seem not to understand and she herself can hardly discern it:

> Earlier in life Hester had vainly imagined that she herself might be the destined prophetess, but had long since recognized the impossibility that any mission of divine and mysterious truth should be confided to a woman stained with sin, bowed down with shame, or even burdened with a life-long sorrow. The angel and apostle of the coming revelation must be a woman, indeed, but lofty, pure, and beautiful; and wise, moreover, not through dusky grief, but the ethereal medium of joy; and showing how sacred love should make us happy, by the truest test of a life successful to such an end!

Ambiguously, Hester's prophecy reminds us of her fallen past. It highlights her limitations not only by its vagueness, but by the traces it suggests of her former radicalism and her lingering sense of martyrdom. Ironically, however, it also points hopefully *through* her limitations toward the future. Hester's anticipation of a new moral order reminds us that she is speaking here with a wisdom deeper than she knows—in Bushnell's terms, a "high constructive instinct" that reaches, indirectly, undesigningly, to antebellum "sentimentality" and Hawthorne's own creed of "sacred love."[11] *Indirectly, undesigningly:* for of course the agency of process is not Hester herself. It is the devious pattern of national history that she unconsciously represents and within which she is an "unexpected forerunner." And central to that pattern, the historical act that most clearly binds Hawthorne's "Introductory" to the narrative proper—the event that most fully validates Hester's final exorcism of the Old World "demons" of revolt; at the end most firmly joins her vision of love to Dimmesdale's forecast for New Israel; and (midway through the novel) best explains Hawthorne's prophetic gloss on the midnight revelation of the A, when under "the muffled sky" a light of supernatural radiance illuminates the familiar scene, lending "another moral interpretation to the things of this world than they had ever borne before" (250–51)—is the American Revolution. Indeed, it is not too much to say that, together with adultery, the Revolution is the novel's fundamental donnée. Adultery is ambiguous pretext and issues in the wrong kind of rebellion; the Revolution is the ironic postscript and vindicates the role of process in an adulterated world.

The vindication is prospective as well as retrospective. It applies no less to the adulterated world of the customshouse than to Puritan New England. As I noted in the last chapter, the conspicuous absence of the word "adultery" facilitates a certain kind of interpretation, one through which a problem in social accountability is "deepened" into a process of symbolic perspective—so, too, with regard to historical perspective, in the case of the American Revolution; only here Hawthorne does break the silence, briefly, in the introduction. "The British army in its flight from Boston," he reports, had discarded as worthless the "packet" containing the letter, and the "ancient yellow parchment," tied up in "faded red tape," had "remained ever since unopened" (143–45). Seventeen seventy-six thus serves to confirm the letter's venerable antiquity ("Prior to the Revolution"), its rare value as a native artifact (the British had "carried off" most "earlier documents"), and its heuristic significance (143–45), leading forward from Hester to Surveyor Pue (whose given name, Jonathan, casts him on the American side, against the Royalist John Bull) to Hawthorne, and more generally from the Puritan forefathers through their latter-day heir to us: "I, the present writer, as their representative, hereby take their shame upon myself for their sakes, and pray that any curse incurred upon them [by their acts of persecution] may be now and henceforth removed" (127).

The anecdote is crucial to the novel's ironic design. It transforms disruption and discontinuity, the *possible* narrative of the A, into a historical chain of providences of which the Revolution is the pivotal link. As a symbol of what the British left behind, the A sanctifies the legacy of the Puritans, prefigures the pattern of Hester's flight, justifies the wisdom of her return, and validates the spirit, if not the letter, of her prophecy. It amounts to a figural endorsement of Hawthorne's strategy of reconciliation.

This is not to confuse irony with biblical typology. Hawthorne was a complex progressive-conservative whose ironies cut both ways, against past and present alike, and, if anything, more fiercely against the present than the past. "The Custom-House" introduction presents America at mid-century as a society that has degenerated "morally, as well as materially" (161)—a free market economy of rights without obligations; a political "spoils system" of obligation without integrity; a cult of the New built on "celestial" humbug.[12] Nostalgia, from this perspective, is part of the novel's work of culture, and the power of nostalgia—ironically, for no epithet comes more readily in connection with Hawthorne's Puritans than "intolerant"—derives from his emphasis on interpretation. Significantly, the novel begins with an act of interpretation, or rather with a series of interpretations. Neither Hester nor Dimmesdale nor Pearl is the novel's interpretive hero; the Puritan community is. The A embodies the viewpoint of the New England leaders, who have decided not to apply the letter of the law—death for adultery—but instead to define it through the ambiguities of mercy and justice. And the ambiguities are promptly drawn out through a variety of redefinitions: by the five fundamentalist matrons who insist (from different perspectives) on the scriptural letter; by the frail young woman who urges charity alone; and by the silent majority, with its latent diversity of views—a diversity that becomes increasingly vocal in the course of the story.

"Harsh," "stern," and "severe" though these Puritans are (207, 212), their strength lies not in coercion but, on the contrary, in their susceptibility to reassessment and change: reassessment of perspective, change of heart, and, hence, capacity for development. In the previous chapter I spoke of *The Scarlet Letter* as a guide to the perplexities of pluralist exegesis. This holds true not only of the novel's authorial directives but of the community it presents. Hawthorne's Puritans are (as it were, despite themselves) a model of gradualist, multivocal interpretation: interpretation among individuals, social groups, and economic classes; across generations; and between ruler and subject, judge and plaintiff. Morally, interpretation combines "gravity" with compassion; aesthetically, it elicits the evolving many meanings of "facts as they exist"; politically, it expresses the "great and warm heart" of "the people" in its rhythms of unity and dispersal; and from all of these angles it justifies Dimmesdale's unspoken decision not to leave, and Hester's to return. More than anything else, it is that Puritan capacity for revaluation that helps "relieve the darkening close of a tale of human frailty and sorrow." And more than any other historical technique, it is that use of shifting perspectives that makes for the extraordinary force of community in *The Scarlet Letter.* Hawthorne never managed this again, for all his intimate knowledge of Holgrave's Salem, his experience at Brook Farm, and his voluminous Italian, English, and American notebooks. This is not because he was more at home in the past than in the present (he was not), and certainly not because he was an advocate of theocracy, but because he found in the connection between liberal and Puritan hermeneutics his own richest access to the ironies of American history.

The Scarlet Letter presents the New England theocracy as a primitive model of pluralist interpretation, in the double sense of primitive, as primal (something essential, foundational) and as antiquated (something to be superseded), "ancient principle" and "ancient prejudice" entwined. And from that ironic viewpoint it offers Hester's tragic story as the remedy by indirection for an era of conflict. Hawthorne rendered Puritan intolerance more vividly than any other historical novelist. And, better than any other, he understood that their intolerance was bound up with certain distinct advantages the Puritans enjoyed *as an interpretive community* over modern liberalism—among these, a "granite" moral code on which to build forms of due process for a community committed to growth; an objective truth through which to stabilize the decentralized, potentially anarchic search for meaning; and a prophetic absolute in which to ground appeals for progress. By the mid-nineteenth century all these sources of authority seemed relics of an outgrown Biblicism. As Hawthorne tells us, the old faith had given way to moral relativism, and, as the novel itself demonstrates, prophecy could serve only metaphorically now, as one of many possible ways of seeing, while truth attracted most by negation, as a partial explanation to be improved upon or at best as the promise of a unity still to be revealed. Hawthorne's art is premised on these changes; his very concept of ambiguity depends on them. But he *also* requires us to recognize, historically, the disadvantages they entail. What has been lost through secularization—what had weakened or dissipated in the gradual (and on the whole beneficial) development from colony to nation—was the moral, prophetic, and intellectual basis of pluralist interpretation that had empowered the course of progress all along.

This ironic appeal to the past was a leitmotif of the era. "Our fathers were not faultless," writes the anonymous author of *The Salem Belle* (1842), and we have improved upon their customs and practices, "but as a community, a nobler race was never seen on the globe." The nostalgia for Puritan New England as for the antidote to current ills was a main theme of virtually every form of popular literature: bicentennial commemorations of the country's origins (such as Emerson's Concord address of 1836) and dedicatory speeches for the founding of various colonial societies (from the 1820s on); catechisms on the cultural verities of the new nation ("Who, then, was the author, inventor and discoverer of independence? The only true answer must be the first [Puritan] emigrants"); July Fourth orations, South as well as North, which can be said to have ritualized the causal relation of Puritanism to independence (indeed, to "every step . . . of American progress . . . as we advance in their history," as orators in Watertown, Massachusetts; Charlestown, South Carolina; Cincinnati, Ohio; and Natchez, Mississippi, variously put it, in 1828, 1839, and 1841); introductions to the numerous printings and reprintings of Puritan writings, such as Thomas Robbins's popular 1820 edition of Cotton Mather's *Magnalia Christi Americana* (1702), which became an important source for Melville, Stowe, and Thoreau (along with a host of historians, politicians, and clergymen); the countless handbooks for "new Americans"—almost three million at mid-century, proportionately the heaviest influx of immigrants in American history—in which the Puritans figured not only as *the* model settlers but as the foil to the perceived dangers of Catholicism (from Irish, German, and Italian immigrants); and the entire genre of "Textbooks on American History for Schoolchildren" that flowered in the 1840s, whose explicit intention it was "to enhance the affection" of "future generations" for the "grand progress from the Puritan fathers to the founders of our country." Nostalgia often slides here into mere filiopietism–laments for "an age of heroic piety, of manly principle, a Golden Age after which the nineteenth-century present seems puny and insignificant." In this time of trial, went the refrain, let us remember that

> Puritanism, Protestantism, and True Americanism are only different terms to designate the same set of principles. . . . [T]hose were Puritan colonies which shaped the early destinies of our country; they were Puritan orators whose spiritual lightning flashed through the masses of the people, and kindled all it touched–and he was a Puritan who led our armies to victory. A Puritan Assembly produced the Declaration, and the Confederation was Puritan in all its principles, and all its aims. Puritanism belongs not to New England only: it is found wherever a heart throbs with genuine American feeling.[13]

This metaphorical use of Puritanism, in which Washington appears as "our great Puritan statesman" (somewhat in the manner of Timothy Dwight's *Conquest of Canaan*, in which he appears as the American Joshua), is the expression in extremis of the figural legacy of early New England. Perhaps the most critical Jacksonian adaptation of that heritage–which is to say, the most ambivalent form of Puritan nostalgia–comes in the procession of historical romances, from Catherine Maria Sedgwick's *Hope Leslie* (1827) and John Neal's *Rachel Dyer* (1828) to James Kirke Paulding's *The Puritan and His Daughter* (1849) and Motley's *Merry Mount* (1849), all of which polarize the Puritans into persecutors and precursors, the villains against whom America defines itself and the heroes from whom the nation derives.* Hawthorne builds on that tradition. What dis-

*The pattern applies even to those novels that recent critics have found most subversive, such as Lydia Maria Childs's *Hobomok: A Tale of Early Times*,

tinguishes him as historian from his contemporaries lies not in his intellectual or aesthetic detachment but, on the contrary, in the depth of his cultural engagement and, through this, his extraordinary understanding of the dynamics of Puritan thought.

We might theorize these dynamics, as Hawthorne understood them, as the hermeneutical unconscious. Although, in his view, the Puritans could not have known it—although they themselves would have abhorred the prospect—group pluralism in America had its first formulation in the colonial theocracy, where it served to sanctify the pristine forms of liberal free enterprise. It is crucial to his view that New England Puritanism was more than a state of mind. It was also for him a distinctly protomodern way of life—a commercial venture undertaken mainly by the mobile "middling classes," a contractual, profit-making "enterprise" whose leaders were virtually all professionals (lawyers, merchants, and university-educated clergymen), men like Governor Bellingham—"bred a lawyer, and accustomed to speak of Bacon, Coke, Noye, and Finch, as his professional associates," and now "transformed" by "the exigencies of this new country . . . into a . . . statesman and ruler" (208). This sense of Puritan pragmatics is basic to Hawthorne's view of his "progenitors" (126). If he sees them antagonistically, as a peculiar brand of religious fanatics, he sees through their fanaticism to the community he repeatedly calls "the people of New England," a self-declared, voluntarily conjoined "little nation" whose principal modes of organization entailed a Hobbist-Calvinist mandate for consensus through legal arbitration,

which assumes that the Puritan "founders," "dark, discontented bigots" though they are, "possessed excellencies, which peculiarly fitted them for a van-guard in the proud and rapid march of freedom" (ed. C. Karcher [1824; reprint, New York: Garrett Press, 1970], 48, 7); and even to such decidedly non–New England novels as James Fenimore Cooper's *The Wept of Wish-Ton-Wish* (1829), where the patriarchal Puritan Mark Heathcote serves as an exemplary founding father.

contractualism, and "open dispute,"[14] as in the famous case he recalls—significantly, just before Hester brings her suit for Pearl to Bellingham—of Goody Sherman versus Captain Robert Keayne: "a dispute concerning the right of property in a pig, [which] not only caused a fierce and bitter contest in the legislative body of the colony, but resulted in an important modification of the framework itself of the legislature" (203–4).

There is no need to rehearse the details of this "famous colonial litigation"—as it has been hailed by legal historians, from the antebellum scholar John Palfrey to Samuel Eliot Morrison and Mark De Wolfe Howe—which issued first in the concept of bicameral legislature and then in the "constitutional doctrine [of "separation of powers"] which is still our inheritance." Suffice it to accent the features that Hawthorne himself suggests: the recourse in *this* community of a poor widow against a prominent merchant; the centrality of the law (in terms of contestation and revision) and the close relation in this respect of legal, religious, commercial, and legislative processes; and above all the remarkable propensity for change, amounting to a standing invitation to reassessment, renegotiation, and readaptation. It is what Tocqueville stressed in *Democracy in America* when he wrote that the entire history of the country was implicit in the Great Migration, as the human race in Adam:

> It must not be imagined that the piety of the Puritans was merely speculative, taking no notice of the course of worldly affairs. Puritanism . . . was almost as much a political theory as a religious doctrine. . . . In England the nucleus of the Puritan movement continued to be in the middle classes, and it was from those classes that most of the emigrants sprang. The population of New England grew fast, and while in their homeland men were still despotically divided by class hierarchies, the colony came more and more to present the novel phenomenon of a society homogeneous in all its parts. Democracy more perfect than any of which antiquity had dared to dream sprang full-grown and fully armed from the midst of the old feudal society. . . . [N]owhere was the principle of liberty applied more completely than in the states of New England . . . [so that it] is often difficult, when

studying the earliest historical and legislative records of New England, to detect the link connecting the immigrants with the land of their forefathers. . . .

All the general principles on which modern constitutions rest, principles which most Europeans in the seventeenth century scarcely understood and whose dominance in Great Britain was then far from complete, are recognized and given authority by the laws of New England; the participation of the people in public affairs, the free voting of taxes, the responsibility of government officials, individual freedom, and trial by jury—all these things were established without question and with practical effect.

These pregnant principles were there applied and developed in a way that no European nation has yet dared to attempt. . . . [I regard this Puritan] origin of the Americans, what I have called their point of departure, as the first and most effective of all the elements leading to their prosperity. The chances of birth [i.e., the Plymouth and Boston migrations] favored the Americans; their [Puritan] fathers of old brought to the land in which they live that equality . . . from which, as from its natural source, a democratic republic was one day to arise. But that is not all; with a republican social state they bequeathed to their descendants the habits, ideas, and mores best fitted to make a republic flourish. When I consider all that has resulted from this first fact, I think I can see the whole destiny of America contained in the first Puritan who landed on these shores, as that of the whole human race in the first man.[15]

Tocqueville's view is disputable, of course, especially in the extreme form it takes. I quote it at length because it so clearly conveys the myth of national beginnings propounded by his Jacksonian hosts. It was from them essentially that he learned the rhetoric of "the Americans," the "origin" and "destiny of America," and the moral-symbolic division between "European" and "American," as between an Old World "despotically divided by class hierarchies" and a New World dedicated to "the principle of liberty." From them Tocqueville heard the creation story of the "fathers of old" who gave "birth," like Zeus to Athena (albeit unknowingly), to "a democratic republic" so different from anything in England that there would appear to be no "link connecting the immigrants with the land of their forefathers." Through their eyes he saw a "United States [in which] there is no religious hatred because religion is universally respected and no sect is predominant; there is no class hatred because the people is everything . . . and finally there is no public distress to exploit because . . . man has only to be left to himself to work marvels." From these narratives Tocqueville inferred the continuities of the errand from East to West–the "gradual and continuous progress" across "the empty continent" (to quote one of Emerson's favorite passages from *Democracy*) and "towards the Rocky Mountains . . . [with] the solemnity of a providential event . . . like a deluge of men rising unabatedly and daily driven onward by the hand of God."[16] And from these same sources, finally, Tocqueville learned about the foundational connection between Puritanism as "religious doctrine" and as "political theory"–which is to say, about the ironies that rendered those colonial sectarians the harbingers of the modern state, replete (as he puts it) with "the habits, ideas, and mores best fitted to make a republic flourish."

Perhaps most striking in this respect–the most telling sign of Tocqueville's debt to the clichés of the culture he was studying–lies in his focus on the law. "Nothing is more peculiar or instructive," he tells us, regarding the Puritans' unconscious modernism, "than the legislation of the time; there, if anywhere, is the key to the social enigma presented to the world by the United States now." On the one hand, the immigrants brought with them a criminal code that was "strongly marked by narrow sectarian spirit," as in "the severity of the penalties for adultery"–the code of a "rough, half-civilized people." On the other hand, they brought "a body of political laws, closely bound up with the penal law, which, though drafted two hundred years ago, still seems very far in advance of the spirit of freedom of our own age." It is a paradigmatically ironic situation (progressive "political laws, closely bound up with the penal law" of "half-civilized" sectarians), and to illustrate its grand issue ("the originality of American civilization")

Tocqueville cites the 1650 Body of Laws. The Puritan code contained such barbarisms as death for adultery, he reports—adding for emphasis a story remarkably parallel to Hester's, of an adulteress who came "very near being sentenced to death"—and then concludes:

The Code states: "It being one chief project of that old deluder, Satan, to keep men from the knowledge of the scriptures, as in former times, keeping them in an unknown tongue, so in these latter times, by persuading them from the use of tongues, so that at least, the true sense and meaning of the original might be clouded with false glosses. . . ." Provisions follow establishing schools in all townships, and obliging the inhabitants, under penalty of heavy fines, to maintain them. . . . No doubt the reader has noticed the preamble to these regulations; in America it is religion which leads to enlightenment and the observance of divine laws which leads men to liberty.[17]

Again, I present Tocqueville's observations not for their accuracy but for their parallels with Bushnell and Bancroft (as quoted above) and, more largely, for their relevance to the dominant Jacksonian view of the culture's development. Let us say that that view contains a certain truth; that it was a truth couched in irony; that the irony provided what we might call the theory of the divine right of pluralist interpretation; that it was a theory (concerning "the observance of the divine laws which lead men to liberty") particularly appropriate to a period of Constitutional debate under a "government by law"; and that the tensions of that period, so conceived, find their most complex and powerful articulation in *The Scarlet Letter.* Hawthorne presents us with the inner narrative of the continuities to which Tocqueville alludes. The opening scaffold scene is one example. As I noted, the process of interpretation that issues in the scarlet letter is at once absolutist and diverse, tempering authoritarianism with a pragmatic, particularized, and relatively open series of deliberations. "The magistrates are God-fearing gentlemen, but merciful overmuch" is the view of one faction of the Puritan community concerning the A (162), and Hawthorne uses the entire scene to elaborate that sense of pliancy, simultaneous with Puritan intolerance. His image here of Puritan judgment is not (as is often said) the sermon on sin. It is a debate about who should try to persuade Hester to confess, in which "kind and genial" John Wilson defers to Dimmesdale as one who knows her "natural temper better than I . . . [and so] could the better judge what arguments to use, whether of tenderness or terror" (173). All Christians assume the complementarity of justice and mercy, but Hawthorne's Puritans further assume, as the vehicle of complementarity, a distinctive form of interpretation, one that centers on the personal "case of conscience," which involves a dissonance of viewpoints and projects (as the end of disputation) a consensus that will in some fundamental way express what Hester accurately perceives to be "the larger and warmer heart of the multitude" (173).

Hawthorne sustains that ironic relation between pluralism and consent through all his various images of Puritan judgment, including the most negative. I think in particular of the scene in which Hester sees her A reflected, "exaggerated and gigantic," in the convex mirror of Bellingham's "gleaming armour" (208). By all accounts it is the novel's most vivid rendering of Puritan bigotry, and as such it has properly been compared with two equally memorable images that precede it. One of these comes at the end of the previous chapter, where Hawthorne tells us, concerning Pearl, that

> neighbouring townspeople . . . seeking vainly elsewhere for the child's paternity, and observing some of her odd attributes, had given out that poor little Pearl was a demon offspring; such as, ever since old Catholic times, had occasionally been seen on earth, through the agency of their mothers' sin, and to promote some foul and wicked purpose. Luther, according to the scandal of his monkish enemies, was a brat of that hellish breed; nor was Pearl the only child to whom this inauspicious origin was assigned, among the New England Puritans. (202)

A much earlier but more direct precedent for the distorted A comes in "Endicott and the Red Cross" (1838), in which Hawthorne first conceptualized Hester:

reflected in the polished breastplate of John Endicott [were] the whipping post . . . the pillory . . . the stocks . . . [and various] individuals . . . sentenced to undergo . . . various modes of ignominy. . . . There was likewise a young woman, with no mean share of beauty, whose doom it was to wear the letter A on the breast of her gown in the eyes of all the world, and her own children.[18]

Critics have exaggerated this symbol of Puritan bigotry, in both the story and the novel, to gigantic proportions, but in fact the twin letters testify to the consistency of Hawthorne's complex progressivism. In the story this manifests itself as a double act of intolerance (the imposing of the A and the rending of the Red Cross) carried out by popular consensus in a spirit of self-righteousness, willfulness, violence, and independence that marks the unconscious beginnings of the American Revolution. In the novel the irony is more fully developed. When Hawthorne attributes to the townspeople the "old Catholic" concept of "demon offspring," he is criticizing them not for being Puritans but for not being Puritan enough. We expect such "superstitions" from the old Catholics, but *they* should have known better, not just because Luther himself had been victim to the same persecution but, more generally, because, as heir to the Lutheran Reformation, Puritanism had effectually replaced medieval hermeneutics with a higher principle of exegesis; in the words of Hawthorne's contemporaries, they had replaced the "enforced allegories of the Romish Church" with "personal interpretation" and "opened the Bible" to the "soul and conscience of each believer," thus reconstituting the Church into a "fellowship of believers by faith alone" that mirrored the simultaneous "variety and unity of Truth itself."

On this basis the transcendentalist reformer William Henry Channing predicted that "Protestantism, or Individualism" would be "the miracle worker" for "our age of conflict," and the conservative professor John Williamson Nevin, reviewing Tocqueville's *Democracy in America,* explained that the Reformation offered a "new stadium . . . in progress for the universal life of the world; having for its object now [in this "republic founded on . . . individual liberty"] the full assertion of what may be styled the *subjective pole of freedom.*" As usual, Bancroft offered the mainstream historical overview:

> the Protestant reformation, considered in its largest influence on politics, was the common people awakening to freedom of mind. . . . [Luther's] principle contained a democratic revolution. . . . At his bidding, truth leaped over the cloister walls, and challenged every man to make her his guest; aroused every intelligence to acts of private judgment . . . lifted each human being out of the castes of the Middle Age, to endow him with individuality, and summoned him to stand forth as man. The world heaved with the fervent conflict of opinion. . . . Luther opened a new world in which every man was his own priest, his own intercessor. . . . Did Luther look to the newly discovered world as the resting place of his teachings? He certainly devised and proposed the rules for emigration. . . . He advised the oppressed . . . to follow "the star" of freedom to lands where religious liberty could find a home. . . . From Luther to Calvin, there was progress; from Geneva to New England, there was more.[19]

Hence the bipolar image of Puritan judgment (demon offspring, Keayne versus Sherman) that precedes Hester's arrival at Bellingham's mansion. Each of these acts of interpretation is a representation of ancient prejudice and ancient principle entwined; each suggests the unexpected means through which history moves forward. Anticipating her confrontation with Puritan law, Hester envisions an "unequal match between the public, on the one side, and a lonely woman . . . on the other" (204). And so it is from one perspective, as from one perspective the dehumanizing A indeed reflects the Puritans' obsession with sin. But, as it turns out, she meets with a diverse group of men who are genuinely, if overzealously, concerned with Pearl's "temporal and eternal welfare"; who not only permit but encourage Hester to speak for herself; who, seeking to "consider weightily" and "judge warily," are careful to examine the child herself (through the Reverend Wilson, "a grandfatherly sort of personage, and usually a vast favorite with children"); and by means of whose collective "counsel and arbitration," finally, Governor Bellingham—as a lawyer attuned to "the exigencies of this new world" and after having heard arguments pro and con—decides, first, *not* to take Pearl from her mother and, then, to take measures to ensure that "at a proper season . . . [she can] go both to school and to meeting" (212–16).

This is not a defense of Puritanism; it is an ironic view of the role of Puritanism in American history. *The Scarlet Letter* assumes a cultural continuum, leading from protoliberal Protestantism to quasi-Protestant liberalism: at one end, a society based on the principles of *sola scriptura* and *sola fides*—committed, that is, both to the Bible's all-sufficiency and to the right of each believer to discover its meanings privately, on the premise that all private meanings, so discovered, would in some measure express cosmic truth—and, at the other end of the continuum, a society dedicated to the principles of free enterprise and the Constitution, on the premise that personal rights would work for the general good, just as the many interpretations of the Constitution would issue in consensus. In both cases the authority is at once legal and textual; in both the appeal is to the individual; and in both the connection between individuals—the communal bond, whether by contract or covenant—centers on the process of interpretation. This process for Hawthorne becomes the "key" (as Tocqueville put it, without being able to explain) to the "enigma" of cultural continuity. From the 1650 Body of Laws (and earlier) through the Constitution, interpretation in these terms had been a chief mode of hegemony. By 1850 the divisions in the country threatened a breakdown of what seemed the very principles of community to those whose hegemony it was. Hawthorne laments this decline as a loss of internal resources, beginning in a failure of historical perspective—specifically, the recognition (to cite Tocqueville again) that "in America it is religion which leads to enlightenment and the observance of divine laws which leads men to liberty"—and he makes it the office of the scarlet letter to reconstitute that perspective in all its ironic implications.

Hester Prynne does not grasp these implications until the end, but Hawthorne, as I suggested, prods his readers toward them from the first scaffold scene. As the crowd gathers, its mood "sombre and grave" and tinged with "awe," he makes us feel *through* Hester's "leaden affliction" the moral power of Puritan consensus:

> The witnesses of Hester Prynne's disgrace had not yet passed beyond their pristine simplicity. They were stern enough to look upon her death, had that been the sentence, without a murmur at its severity, but they had none of the heartlessness of another social state, which would find a theme for jest in an exhibition like the present. (166)

The juxtaposition of bigotry and simplicity—"pristine simplicity"—is characteristic of Hawthorne's portrait of the settlers. Here as elsewhere, he intends it as a contrast with the bigotry of his own time: the "heartless" system of party patronage, in which victors, he tells us in the introduction, not only axe the adversary but "ignominiously . . . kick the head which they have just struck off" (154). And, here as elsewhere, the contrast is meant to evoke some vital source of community. In "The Gray Champion" he embodies this resource in an atavistic principle of intolerance that (he tells us) has animated each successive step to independence, culminating in the Revolution. In *The Scarlet Letter*, as in Tocqueville's *Democracy*, that principle involves *both* the Puritans' moral rigidity *and* their capacity for change, on all levels of theocracy, and in this ambiguous sense it finds its fullest expression in the colonists' response to Dimmesdale's election day sermon:

> There was a momentary silence, profound as what should follow the utterance of oracles. Then ensued a murmur . . . [and at last, in] the

open air, their rapture broke into speech. The street and the market-place absolutely babbled.

Now was heard again the clangor of music, and . . . the train of venerable and majestic fathers were seen moving through a broad pathway of the people. When they were fairly in the market-place, their presence was greeted by a shout. This—though doubtless it might acquire additional force and volume from the childlike loyalty which the age awarded its rulers—was felt to be an irresistible outburst of the enthusiasm kindled in the auditors. . . . Each felt the impulse in himself, and, in the same breath, caught it from his neighbor. . . . There were human beings enough, and enough of highly wrought and symphonious feeling, to produce that more impressive sound than the organ-tones of the blast, or the thunder, or the roar of the sea; even that mighty swell of many voices, blended into one great voice by the universal impulse which makes likewise one vast heart out of the many. (333–34)

That choral shout of affirmation in the "open air" of the marketplace, articulating what "each felt . . . in himself," is surely one of the memorable moments in the utopian strain that critics have identified with classic American literature. Ironically, the very elements that distance us from the Puritans—their street "babble," their eagerness for "oracles"—contribute to the power we feel in the "rapture" of their "united testimony." What begins as a condescending metaphor of organic development ("childlike loyalty") grows into a consummate figure of hope. It recalls the novel's opening allusion to utopia. It makes incarnate, if only for an instant, the transformation promised midway through the narrative, when the A flashes in "strange and solemn splendor" across the midnight sky, "as if it were the . . . daybreak that shall unite all who belong to one another." Through its very archaism, the Puritans' "childlike loyalty" requires us to interpret them—historically, as a theocracy—in the light of Romantic Neoplatonism: childhood as the state closest to the divine fount. It is the providential unconscious made manifest in "symphonious feeling": an "irresistible outburst" that sounds more impressively "than the thunder, or the roar of the sea." Rising above the loyalties of "the age," this infant "people," united in the marketplace by a "universal impulse which makes one vast heart out of the many," stands as a sweeping reproof to the mature marketplace republic satirized in "The Custom-House."

It is a reproof shot through with irony. From first to last Hawthorne plays upon our recognition of the *advantages* of the past from which we have (providentially) *advanced.* And that recognition posits more than an unintended national legacy. It suggests the intrinsic connections within Puritanism itself between morality, religious certainty, and prophetic faith. These are the connections underlying the legal and marketplace continuities that Tocqueville could not provide, though they are intimated in the very language of the passage he quotes. I refer to the Hartford Code of 1650 (following upon the case of Keayne v. Sherman), with its emphasis on Scripture interpretation and, in these terms, its progressivist contrast between Satan's work then, "in former times," and now, "in these latter times," when we have reached a "true sense and meaning" to counteract the old "false glosses."

The sensitivity of Hawthorne's contemporaries to such intimations can be traced throughout the literature; they are intrinsic to the ironic view of history. Their import for *The Scarlet Letter* in particular warrants a brief explanation. The colonists, Hawthorne understood, believed that their nonconformity placed them at the vanguard of God's grand design. Truth for them was, of course, one and indivisible, and sectarianism was a sign of the adulterated human condition. But the adulteration, though absolute in kind, was relative in time. Words could bring them closer to the Word, successive revelations of meaning nearer to the truth. That step-by-step progress rendered interpretation a central aspect of the spiral of sacred history, of which the acme was "these latter times"—an age of "signs and wonders" leading gradually to the "unsealing of all the mysteries of *Scripture*, even unto the Whole of REVELATIONS." A favorite Puritan image for this fusion of process and telos was God's summons to His "peculiar people" to rebuild "the temple of the Lord" in preparation for the Second Coming. Samuel Danforth made the image central to his *Brief Recognition of New England's Errand into the Wilderness* (1670), the election day sermon on which Hawthorne modeled Dimmesdale's address of 1649. The biblical event also served in this figural perspective to explain the polemical, divisive tendencies of Puritan interpretation:

> there . . . must be many schisms and many dissections made in the quarry and in the timber, ere the house of God can be built. And when every stone is laid artfully together, it cannot be untied [absolutely] . . . it can but be contiguous in this world; neither can every piece of the building be of one form; nay rather the perfection consists in this, that out of many moderate varieties and brotherly dissimilitudes that are not vastly disproportional, arises the goodly and the graceful symmetry that commends the whole pile and structure.
>
> Let us, therefore, be more considerate builders, more wise in spiritual architecture, when great reformation is expected. For now the time seems come, wherein *Moses*, the great prophet, may sit in heaven rejoicing to see that memorable and glorious wish of his fulfilled, when not only our seventy elders, but all the Lord's people, are become prophets.[20]

This passage argues for tolerance to a degree that most colonial leaders felt they could not permit in practice, but the argument itself, advocating a hermeneutics "contiguous" in application because it is proleptic in principle, expressed the premises of the New England Way.* Indeed, that Way appropriated the gen-

*I have chosen my examples from John Milton's *Areopagitica* (1644) and John Cotton's *Exposition upon the Thirteenth Chapter of the Revelation* (1642) in order to suggest (1) the broad transatlantic base of this tendency in Puritan hermeneutics, (2) its distinctive New England applications, and (3) the line of New England apocalyptic leading from the first generation to the next, Cotton to Danforth (and beyond). Among the many New England Puritans I might have selected, Cotton has particular relevance here, first, because recent scholarship suggests that he was a prototype for Dimmesdale (Michael J. Colacurcio, "The Footsteps of Anne Hutchinson," *ELH* 39 [1972]: 459–94), and, more importantly, because his sermon on Revelation 13—delivered before Boston's faction-ridden "UNITED SYNOD of Churches"—is an exemplary

eral Protestant rationale for pluralism—diversity within consensual restraints for the purpose of apocalyptic reformation—as *its* "peculiar covenant." These nonseparating congregational schismatics undertook something far more than a "moderate variety" of congregationalism when, as Bushnell reminded his audience of 1849, they set out to advance "the kingdom of Christ in these remote parts of the world." "These remote parts" (or, as the Puritans termed it, "ends of the earth") had a teleological as well as geographical meaning. They signified the latter-day Zion reserved from eternity for a "remnant summoned from afar"—in Dimmesdale's words, for a second Israel "newly gathered" to reverse the "judgments and ruin" visited

instance of the use of teleology to blend pluralism and consensus through the concept of process-as-progress. The factionalism I refer to followed from the antinomian controversy, in which Cotton played an ambiguous role, and he was properly humble. Let us "not be too confident," he pleaded, about our particular interpretations; instead, since "we shall see a further gradual accomplishment and fulfilling of this Prophecy here," let us "search together," remembering that "all things go in a gradation" (*Exposition* [London: Livewell, Chapman, 1655], 93). By "here" Cotton meant the New England annus mirabilis, which he predicted for 1655.

The special relevance of Milton (again, from among many possible English Puritan examples) lies in his importance for Hawthorne's time and beyond. For instance, he figures recurrently in nineteenth-century contrasts between the Great Migration and Cromwell's rebellion, as in James Russell Lowell's introduction to *Areopagitica* (New York: Grolier Club, 1890). Between 1642 and 1649, Lowell reports, England underwent "a universal ferment of thought" in which "every form of mental and moral bewilderment suddenly loosed from the unconscious restraints of traditional order," and, although Milton himself "ventured . . . in that dangerous direction," nonetheless, as author of the *Areopagitica*, he remains a "champion of the doctrines of freedom and democracy," which flow from "our own forefathers" to the Revolutionary "founders" (xix, xxi–xxiv).

The continuities this entails are discussed from a different perspective by Stanley Fish, in comparing H. L. A. Hart's liberal classic, *The Concept of Law* (1961) with Milton's claims for scriptural exegesis in *Areopagitica.* Hart grounds truth in a theory of language, Milton in a vision of God, but for Milton, too, Fish argues, a "sequence that begins with Truth reassuringly presented as a superior and self-validating principle ends with Truth becoming indistinguishable from the forces that contend in her name. . . . [Thus,]

upon Israel of old (332), so that the wilderness might blossom as the rose and Moses rejoice "to see that memorable and glorious wish of his fulfilled." Thus, Winthrop promised the *Arabella* passengers (by the figural authority of Moses) that, if they kept covenant with God, they would "see much more of His wisdom, power, goodness, and truth than formerly." Thus, too, forty years later, Danforth explained that truly to "see" the errand was to re-cognize it progressively, as a process of expanding insight, from the Old Testament to the New, and from the early Church to the New England Way. So perceived—understood comparatively, by gradation, in terms of the still unfolding revelation of Christ—the colonial mission, Danforth assured his audience, was "greater" than others before it because it represented a higher *historical* "dispensation" and therefore a fuller unveiling of things past and to come.[21]

All this is implicit in Dimmesdale's address; to these promises "the people of New England" raise their "irresistible" choral assent. Hawthorne's description seems to me accurate in substance, even though it disregards the factionalism of the 1640s and conflates a first- with a second-generation audience and text. I would only add to it that the vision to which "the people" assent does not express the truth of faith as distinct from metaphors of the imagination. Dimmesdale's rhetoric is

rather than sitting as a judge of conflict she is at once the site and product of conflict" (From an unpublished talk, subsequently expanded as two essays, "Unger and Milton" and "Force," in *Doing What Comes Naturally: Change, Rhetoric, and the Practice of Theory in Literary and Legal Studies* [Durham, N.C.: Duke University Press, 1989], 503–24). This comparison might be restated in terms of what I called the continuum of liberal hermeneutics. For Hart, as for Milton, legal process implies progress, but the implication in Hart's case depends on social precedent and principle, and so remains dependent on the *force* of rhetoric. So it does, too, in Protestant hermeneutics, but force is mystified here—*justified*, in the Calvinist sense—by a telos independent of cultural process. Hawthorne can be said to stand midway between these two points. Skeptical though he is, he retains at least something, as in his use of "providence," of the old *justification* of pluralism as progress.

a prime instance of the aesthetic power of ideology: politics, morality, and the imagination combined, tropes of social cohesion in Truth's clothing. The Judeo-Christian legacy to Puritanism was the rhetorical spoils of a series of self-declared chosen peoples: the language of election through which the ancient Hebrews justified their conquest of Canaan; the biblical typology through which the church fathers laid claim to the entire story of the Hebrews, from Adam to the prophets; and the *clavis apocalypticae* by which the Reformers interpreted Catholicism as the Beast of Rome and themselves as the One True Church. By that authority the Massachusetts Bay colonists claimed the New World "by promise."[22] By that authority they reversed the dependency of the New World on the Old, much as their Old World forebears had reversed *their* dependency on the "heathens" from Homer through Plato, Aristotle, and Virgil, by interpreting them all as unconscious harbingers of Christ. By that authority, finally, the Puritan immigrants reduced the century-long Reformation to a foreshadowing of the Great Migration. Appropriating the Protestant teleology to themselves, they declared their errand to be the climactic mission of the Church; their locale to be the last, best wilderness-to-be-reclaimed; and their interpretations to be more closely attuned than that of any other people to the Truth still to be fully revealed.

That act of appropriation became the visionary dimension of the Puritans' venture into the emergent marketplace world, and their "language of Canaan," accordingly, entered into their unconscious legacy to liberal culture. As recent scholars have shown, "strategies of control" in the early Republic centered on a rhetoric of reconciliation that was rooted both in the ambiguities of legal language and in a providential sense of mission. Reason and experience, according to this bivalent outlook, "participate in a higher truth"; this "truth is a matter of cumulative knowledge (finding the design in diverse components)"; as such, it is the commonsense expression of a transcendent order—Nature's God (Thomas Jefferson), "a superintending Providence in our Favour" (Benjamin Franklin), an "Almighty hand . . . frequently and signally extended to our relief" (James Madison)—and transcendence is manifest as law-to-be-interpreted (process and telos fused) in the Constitution. By 1838 Abraham Lincoln could speak of "reverence for the laws" as "the *political religion* of the nation" (since "in contemplation of universal law, and of the Constitution, the Union of these States is perpetual"); and a year later John O'Sullivan, "inspired by . . . the fresh enthusiasm of a new heaven and a new earth," could declare that the Constitution was "destined to manifest to mankind the excellence of divine principles; to establish on earth the noblest temple ever dedicated to the worship of the Most High." Ritualistically, O'Sullivan traced the process of temple building back to colonial New England: "the powerful purpose of soul, which, in the seventeenth century, sought a refuge among savages, and reared in the wilderness the sacred altars of intellectual freedom. . . . was the seed that produced individual equality, and political liberty, as its natural fruit; and this is our true nationality."[23]

The burden of explanation naturally fell to the historians. In 1841 William Prescott celebrated the belief in pluralist consensus as "this tendency . . . towards republican institutions, which connects Colonial history with that of the Union." "Truth, indeed, is single," he acknowledged, "but opinions are infinitely various, and it is only by comparing these opinions together that we can hope to ascertain what is truth"—in this faith the Revolution was fought, the republican "rule by law" instated, and the Constitution ratified; in this faith, the Puritans established a theocracy that ironically made America the home of "the natural rights of humanity." For "if the first settlers were intolerant in practice, they brought with them the living principle of freedom. . . . They could not avoid it." Prescott was summing up (with admiration and approval) the latest volume of Bancroft's *History of the United States.* Six years earlier Bancroft himself had made much the same connection between hermeneutics and national progress. "Because God is visible in History," he explained, the historian's "office is the noblest . . . of all pursuits that require analysis," but it was an office of indirections and ambiguities:

> Truth is one. . . . [and yet] Truth is not to be ascertained by the impulses of an individual; it emerges from the contradictions of personal opinions; it raises itself in majestic serenity above the strifes of parties and the conflicts of sects. . . . It is alone by infusing great principles into the common mind, that revolutions in human society are brought about. . . . Society can be . . . advanced, only by moral principle diffused through the multitude. . . . The duty of America is to secure the culture and happiness of the masses by their reliance on themselves.[24]

Bancroft was seeking here to define "The Office of the People in Art, Government, and Religion." His definition, like Prescott's, substitutes the secular terms of liberal thought for those of Puritan exegesis: "opinions" for "schisms," "parties" for "dissections," and "the common mind" for "the Lord's people."* Like Prescott, too, he locates the "moral principles" (the

*Bancroft's essay also suggests (what I have been implying all along) that one aspect of the symbology Hawthorne inherited—closely related to its modes of irony and ambiguity—is a distinctive rhetoric of "public office." I refer to the language of democratic representativeness, from the office of the presidency to that of customshouse surveyor, as it developed during the Jacksonian and antebellum periods—a rhetoric that Hawthorne mocks in his introduction to *The Scarlet Letter*, but which he applies there by contrast to his office as artist. I discuss this entire issue in a separate study on the growth of the liberal concept of office. For present purposes, one example must suffice, the theory of the two-party system, as represented by one insider's overview of the debate on "Parties—The Office They Fulfill":

> Party spirit at bottom is but the conflict of different opinions, to each of which some portion of truth almost invariably adheres; and what has ever been the effect of this mutual action of mind upon mind, but to . . . raise the general mind above its former level. [However, since] . . . the forces which are [thus] set in motion are [very] . . . extensive, we must contrive some machinery equally extensive for the purpose of controlling them. And thus popular parties very naturally, not to say necessarily, take the

"duty of America") in the constitutional "Temple of the Law." And, like O'Sullivan, he traces the process of temple building, in its manifold "varieties and brotherly dissimilitudes," back to the "sacred faith," the "civil polity," and the "internal administration" of seventeenth-century New England. That concept of the "origin of the Americans," as Tocqueville put it, was already well in place by 1821, when Martin Luther Hurlbut of Charleston, South Carolina, commemorated the Plymouth landing:

To the heroes of the revolution we owe, indeed, as much as any community can owe to mortal services. . . . But let them not *engross* our gratitude, or admiration. . . . It is not to their exertions, nor to their days, that we are to trace the origin of our civil and political privileges. . . . They did but guard from violation the sacred fire, which they found burning on their paternal altars. The . . . institutions, for the defence of which they jeopardized their lives and shed their blood, were the institutions of . . . [Puritan] New England.

---

place of . . . checks and balances. . . . The true office of parties then is to elicit and make manifest the amount of truth which belongs to the tenets of each, so that the great body of the people . . . may be both easily and understandingly guided in the path they pursue. . . . And ironically . . . the wider the arena in which parties move, the more numerous the persons who compose them, the less dangerous they are to the state. (Frederick Grimké, *The Nature and Tendency of Free Institutions* [1848; reprint Cambridge, Mass.: Harvard University Press, 1968], 172, 174, 178, 175)

Hence, Tocqueville's well-known remark: "In America the two parties agreed on the most essential points. Neither of the two had, to succeed, to destroy an ancient order or to overthrow the whole of a social structure" (*Democracy in America*, ed. J. T. Mayer, trans. George Lawrence [Garden City, N.Y.: Doubleday, 1969], 175). Richard Hofstadter traces that form of agreement to the process of "constitutional consensus" from James Madison through Martin Van Buren (*The Idea of a Party System: The Rise of Legitimate Opposition in the United States, 1780–1840* [Berkeley: University of California Press, 1969], 4, and passim); Jean H. Baker details the practical politics it involved in showing "the ways in which the Northern Democracy, for all its shrill sectarianism, nonetheless served as a nationalizing force" (*Affairs of Party: The Political Culture of Northern Democrats in the Mid-Nineteenth Century* [Ithaca, N.Y.: Cornell University Press, 1983], 10). Both Baker and Hofstadter confirm the "irony" that Grimké emphasizes (187)—that "rotation of office" is "a species of discipline" that "binds together [all] the parts of society."

Some three decades later, deliberately echoing those commonplaces (but not mocking them), Melville called the Constitution "the Bible of the Free" and the Declaration of Independence "the ark of the liberties of the world," borne by "the Israel of our time." All this had come about, he reminded his readers, "not wholly because you in your wisdom decreed it. . . . Nor in their germ are all your blessings to be ascribed to the noble sires who of yore [1776] fought in your behalf. . . . Your ancient pilgrims fathered your liberty."[25]

By mid-century, however, the political religion of New Israel was undergoing a crisis of faith. In part, it was the crisis of an ideology that had worked too well. The "transformation of American law," which confirmed the hegemony of the North, as Morton Horwitz has shown, issued in a narrow professionalism that undermined the universalist claims of liberal rule by law. The fierce debates over the "slavery" hiatus in the Constitution served to confirm the sanctity both of law in general and the Constitution in particular, but they also revealed the bias, arbitrariness, and sheer contrivance inherent in interpretation. These and similar reversals at mid-century were threatening to undo the Union. Something more than legal ambiguity was needed to restore the belief in common enterprise. As Rufus Choate put it, in a widely discussed address in Salem (perhaps with Hawthorne in the audience), the courts could no longer be expected to hold the country together. "The law appeals to the rational faculty in man," he explained, but we need to reach beyond this to "the heart and affections and imaginations of the whole people." We require an "expressive mode" to convey "the truly sacred nature of America's political institutions." To that end he urged "The Importance of Illustrating New England History by a Series of Romances":

> *the old Puritan character* . . . [is] inscribed upon all the sides of our religious, political, and literary edifices, legibly and imperishably. But while we appreciate what the Puritans have done, and recognize the divine wisdom and purposes in raising them up to do it, something

is wanting yet to give to their character and fortunes a warm, quick interest, a charm for the feelings and imagination, an abiding place in the heart and memory and affections of all the generations of the people to whom they bequeathed these representative governments and this undefiled religion. It is time that literature and the arts should at least cooperate with history. . . . Reminded of our fathers, we [will] remember that we are brethren . . . merged in an expanded, comprehensive, constitutional sentiment . . . all tending toward one . . . final, grand, complex result [and thereby] reassembling, as it were, the people of America in one vast congregation.[26]

In a sense *The Scarlet Letter* is the novel that Choate called for. Its romance perspective merges national history with the memory of the Fathers in "an expanded, comprehensive, *constitutional* appeal." I think here first of Hawthorne's plot: the law, embedded in the culture's sacred text (the Bible), generates a conflict of interpretation that the law itself cannot resolve—which, indeed, remains unresolved until Hester resumes the letter beyond legal judgment, or, rather, in a visionary spirit that incorporates the law in the very act of transcending it and so (in Bancroft's terms) expresses "the office of the people in art, government, and religion." Second, I think of the nineteenth-century responses to *The Scarlet Letter:* as literary classic, as "the embodiment of what Americans share, the chief incarnation of the ethos that gives them existence as a people," or, more simply, in Henry James's words, as a "work . . . redolent of the social system in which [Hawthorne] had his being."[27] But the novel's cultural work goes deeper than that. Its historical subject is neither the problem of the law nor the advantages of consensus. It is the process through which liberal society achieves consensus, the ambiguities through which it makes reconciliation seem both inevitable and desirable, a private necessity we cannot help but choose. *The Scarlet Letter* elicits our ironic participation in a romance of the culture's expressive forms. "Participation" in this case means interpretation, and "irony" a set of historiographical directives through which we harness our capacities for empathy, insight, analysis, and appreciation—our "critical faculties" in all their multivalent subjectivity—to a certain continuum of interpretive theory and practice. At one end of that continuum there is Hester amidst the Puritans, 1642–49 (Hester "the hidden one," as her name implies, the secret rebel who most fully appeals to our subjectivity); at the other end is the ironic reader in the text, returned with Hawthorne to the past in order to relive the A-history of pluralist hermeneutics.

Chapter Three

The Red Badge of Compromise

"THE SCARLET LETTER had not done its office": Hawthorne's devious, multivalent directive has behind it the authority of all the cultural forces that were mobilizing to meet the mid-century crisis at home and abroad. In suggesting that he did more than write the romance that Choate had called for, I had in mind not only Hawthorne's uses of the past but also his engagement with the anxieties of the moment. For present purposes, they may be described through two far-reaching events—one external, the European Forty-eight, and the other internal, the compromise through which North and South hoped to avoid civil war. Both events gathered momentum through the previous decade (in America a period of widening regional divisions, in Europe the dawn of revolutionary socialism); both events seemed to be resolved by 1852 (with the election of Franklin Pierce and the restoration of European monarchy); and both are implicit in the letter's office. Once again Hawthorne himself suggests the connection—this time in the poignant passage in "The Custom-House" when he takes up the "rag of scarlet cloth," places it on his breast, feels its "burning heat," and "shuddering," drops it to the floor (145–46). It amounts to an emblem play of authorial identification, balancing distance and empathy, pointing backward from Hawthorne to Hester and forward from her cottage threshold to his customshouse office. Hawthorne uses the moment of contact to assert his sense of difference, even as he returns with Hester to colonial Boston and transforms himself—as writer, as victim of party politics, and as a son of the Puritans—into a symbol of continuity. Ideologically, that symbol joins the novel's two time frames: first, the fictional time frame, 1642–49, with its implied contrast between models of revolt (recurrent violence in the Old World, organic progress in the New); and second, the authorial time frame, 1848–52, with its ominous explosion of conflict at home and abroad.

The "red year Forty-eight," as Melville recalled it in *Clarel*, brought "the portent and the fact of war, / And terror that into hate subsides." He was referring to the series of revolutions from which Europe's kings "fled like the gods" (although by 1852 "even as the gods / . . . return they made; and sate / And fortified their strong abodes"). But he might have been referring as well to what New England conservatives considered an ominous tendency toward confrontation following the victory of the Whigs. The presidency of James Polk (1844–48) was a high point of antebellum chauvinism. Mexico had been defeated (yielding the spoils of California, Texas, and New Mexico); the Oregon Territory appropriated (along with Nevada, Arizona, Colorado, and parts of Utah); record waves of immigrants absorbed; gold discovered in the West; the entire Great Lakes region (including several million acres of "open" land "confiscated from the Indians"); Florida, Texas, Iowa, and Wisconsin admitted to the Union; and plans devised to extend "commercial and territorial advantages beyond the continent" to Yucatán, Cuba, Hawaii, China.[1]

Then in 1848 Polk's unexpected defeat called attention to long-festering internal divisions. We can see in retrospect how both tendencies, toward expansion and toward confrontation—"unprecedented growth," "irreconcilable conflict"—expressed the same process of ideological consolidation.* But for a good many of the disempowered Democrats these tensions of process evoked the "terrors of a European conflagration." It is no accident that Hawthorne would have connected the revolutions abroad with his loss of tenure at the Salem Customs House. As recent scholarship has demonstrated, he links both sets of events in the alternative title he offers for the novel, "THE POSTHUMOUS PAPERS OF A DECAPITATED SURVEYOR" (156), and the political innuendos are expanded from "The Custom-House" introduction to the novel at large, in the recurrent imagery of 1848–49 revolutions, including allusions to scaffold and guillotine.[2]

The authorial time frame, then, opens with the Year of the Red Scare: Chartist agitation in England, the First Paris Commune, *The Communist Manifesto,* and widespread revolt in France, Austria, Germany, Belgium, Prussia, Poland, Bohemia, Rumania, Denmark, Ireland, Italy, Czechoslovakia, and Hungary. Americans at first welcomed these events. They were basically liberal revolutions, after all—"wars of independence, like ours, against the despot and royal tyrant"—and seemed to be proving, in George Duyckinck's words, that "our country leads the world." But after this brief period of euphoria, as liberal leadership failed in one country after another, and collectivist groups (socialist, communist, and others) became increas-

*One indication of this dynamic is the continuing debate about consolidation or conflict in antebellum America. In David Potter's summary: "Some historians argue that Taylor's policy of firmness would have dissolved the crisis and averted the dangers of secessionism. . . . Others contend that the disruptive forces in 1850 were extremely powerful and that the compromise gave the Union another indispensable decade to grow in strength and cohesion" (*The Impending Crisis, 1848–1861*, ed. Don E. Fehrenbacher [New York: Harper and Row, 1976], 118). It is significant in this context how often the argument for slavery was presented as "a policy of laissez-faire against . . . [federal] attempts to interfere" (Rush Welter, *The Mind of America, 1820–1860* [New York: Columbia University Press, 1975], 341) and that Jefferson Davis's inaugural address as president of the seceding Southern states appeals primarily to the traditions of the revolutionary Founding Fathers.

ingly prominent, public opinion turned decisively against the "radicals." Those who did the turning expressed disillusionment in various ways, but common to all was the contrast I described earlier between American and European revolution, as between gradual progress and recurrent violence. By spring 1848, Evert Duyckinck informed his brother George that New Yorkers associated the "agitation" with "recollections of . . . Robespierre"; shortly after, George Bancroft reported that it had Boston "frightened out of its wits"; by early 1849 American conservatives concluded that "republics cannot grow on the soil of Europe." Worse still, they had already observed the incipient effect in America itself of European conflict: the "foreboding shadows," as one journalist put it, of "Communism, Socialism, Pillage, Murder, Anarchy, and the Guillotine vs. Law and Order, Family and Property." Bancroft at first tried to calm his conservative friends–"these insurrections," he urged, were "the echo of American Democracy . . . from France, and Austria, and Prussia, and all Old Germany" and might actually "stir up the hearts of the American people to new achievements"–but he soon conceded that events were tending in just the opposite direction: geographically, from the Old World to the New and, morally, from liberty to license.[3]

License took many forms, as these antebellum Jeremiahs detailed its invasion of America.* A sinister "infusion of Euro-

*My subject is the American response to the events, not the revolutions themselves, but it is worth noting, as an index to that response, that historians have attributed the failure of the European Forty-eight to virtually the same factors that obtained in the American Seventy-six, when liberalism officially triumphed not only in the United States but as "America." According to a standard overview of "The Patterns of 1848," the

> fundamental flaws in each of the [European] risings consisted of the liberal mentality of the revolutionary leaders and the profound social cleavage between the liberal and lower-class forces involved in the revolution. . . .
>
> With rare exceptions none of the men who assumed control of the revolutionary governments had ever been a revolutionary [as was the case in

pean Socialism," they charged, was corroding "the Christian republicanism of America": "crack-brained speculatists who have recently attempted to turn the world upside down . . . have [now] come hither"–"ultraists [who], attempting to advance men in truth and goodness . . . begin by destroying what of these they already possess"; "radicals [who seek] . . . not merely to lop off diseased branches, but for the sake of getting rid of these to uproot . . . the tree itself"; and "Red Republicans" who hope to institute "the principles of the Terrorists . . . on this side of the Atlantic also," and so to "overturn the laws of . . . civilization . . . the tribunal of reason, and the voice of the natural conscience." And all these "bold, unscrupulous," and "reckless" notions, which had "found preachers and proselytes on this side of the Atlantic," seemed to have a common source—a "speculative fanaticism," a "wild freedom of speculation" concerning "all the great subjects of religion, government, political economy, and civil liberty."[4] Hawthorne may

---

1776]. They accepted the upheaval that had brought them to power, but they wanted no further disorder. . . .

Furthermore, liberals had already won some of their goals in many of the countries in which revolution occurred [as they had in 1776 in the thirteen colonies], which limited their rebellion against the status quo. . . . Government was efficient; it encouraged some economic modernization, spread education widely, offered some opportunities to middle-class bureaucrats, permitted a considerable degree of religious freedom, and granted substantial powers to city governments. . . . It is [therefore] possible to see why liberals did not feel a need to press too hard. . . .

The liberals of course represented men of position and property [as they did in 1776], and this also moderated their behavior. . . .

Hence for a variety of reasons the liberal leaders did not do what they would have had to do to make revolution a success. (Peter N. Stearns, *1848: The Revolutionary Tide in Europe* [New York: Norton, 1974], 225–27)

In every case what was a "fundamental flaw" in Europe proved to be a fundamental advantage for the American War of Independence. And the visionary as well as pragmatic strategies that made for the difference—the rhetoric and rituals that allowed "the liberal leaders [of 1776] to do what they had to do to make revolution a success"—by 1848–50 had become a ripened cultural symbology.

be said to condense these and similar charges in his overview of Hester's nihilism:

> She had wandered, without rule or guidance, in a moral wilderness . . . [and] looked from her estranged point of view at human institutions, and whatever priests or legislators had established; criticizing all with hardly more reverence than the Indian would feel for the clerical band, the judicial robe, the pillory, the gallows, the fireside or the church. The tendency of her fate and fortune had been to set her free. *The scarlet letter was her passport into regions where other women dared not tread.* Shame, Despair, Solitude! These had been her teachers,—stern and wild ones,—and they had made her strong, but taught her much amiss. (290; my emphasis)

The taboo regions to which Hawthorne refers had an especially ominous meaning for antebellum conservatives. By virtually all accounts, from the highbrow *North American Review* to the evangelical *Biblical Repertory*, the most pernicious heresies of the European Forty-eight pertained to the domestic sphere. Striking at the very nexus of social order and spiritual values, the radicals were advocating "the abrogation of the family, the breaking up of the fireside circle." They were seeking nothing less than "to *emancipate* woman, by making her independent of man," thus "giving her up to follow her passions" and "making a rule of adultery." And precisely this heresy, through which "all old laws, all ancient morals" are nullified, seemed to be gathering most force in the United States.[5] The "regions where . . . women dared not tread" had of course long been open territory to male terrorists, not only on the continent but also in England, from the early seventeenth-century antinomians to the Chartists of 1848. Even there, however, women had characteristically restrained themselves because, in Hawthorne's account, they intuited that to indulge the "tendency to speculation"—to be "set free" *as women* "without rule or guidance, in a moral wilderness" beyond "Law and Order, Family and Property"—would be to alter their very "natures." It would drain them of the "ethereal essence, wherein [woman] has her truest life."

This explanation directly precedes Hawthorne's reminder that "the scarlet letter had not done its office"; it deserves to be quoted at length, as offering the single most detailed account we have of Hester's secret radical thoughts (as well as the most sustained preview of her final vision of womanhood, after the letter has served its *proper* office as passport back into New England history):

> A dark question often rose into her mind, with reference to the whole race of womanhood. Was existence worth accepting, even to the happiest among them? . . . A tendency to speculation, though it may keep woman quiet, as it does man, yet makes her sad. She discerns, it may be, such a hopeless task before her. As a first step, the whole system of society is to be torn down, and built up anew. Then, the very nature of the opposite sex, or its long hereditary habit, which has become like nature, is to be essentially modified, before woman can be allowed to assume what seems a fair and suitable position. Finally, all other difficulties being obviated, woman cannot take advantage of these preliminary reforms, until she herself shall have undergone a still mightier change, in which, perhaps, the ethereal essence, wherein she has her truest life, will be found to have evaporated. A woman never overcomes these problems by any exercise of thought. They are not to be solved, or only in one way. If her heart chance to come uppermost, they vanish. (260–61)

These were not problems that exercised Anne Hutchinson or Witch Hibbins. Nor did they vex the bold theorists of Cromwell's England. But for Hawthorne, we may assume, those radicals were implicated in the unnatural reforms that Hester contemplates, and her contemplations in turn reflected the "unhealthy" feminism that he had encountered in 1841 at Brook Farm (a prerevolutionary instance, so to speak, of the invasion of European radical ideas) and that he was shortly to mock in *The Blithedale Romance* (1852).*

*To some extent this also includes the prophetic Hester at the end. Insofar as she retains her old rebellious ways, Hester can be said to reflect the image (widely ridiculed in the midcentury press) of the radical female "angel" who would announce the coming revolution, some self-styled "*Woman-Messiah*" who would presume "to reveal the laws . . . of the future" ("Societary Theo-

We may assume, further, that Hawthorne's emphasis on the "dark question . . . of womanhood" was grounded in an event of 1848, which brought all of these radical continuities into focus for him. During the summer of that year, soon after the sensational women's March for Bread at Versailles, the first American Women's Rights Convention opened at Seneca Falls, New York. It was quickly designated the most alarming symptom to date of the "Red plague" in the United States. According to social commentators, reports of "the female 'Reds' of Europe" had already "appalled the American public," and from pulpit, press, and political platform spokesmen for order and due process rushed to make the connection:

> This is the age of revolutions. To whatever part of the world the attention is directed, the political and social fabric is crumbling to pieces; and changes which far exceed the wildest dreams of the enthusiastic Utopians of the last generation, are now pursued with ardor and perseverence. The principal agent, however, that has hitherto taken part in these movements has been the rougher sex . . . [and] though it is asserted that no inconsiderable assistance was contributed by the gen-

ries," *American Whig Review* 7 [June, 1848]: 640)—or, in the words of Albert Brisbane's Fourierist manifesto, "the fully developed . . . independent woman . . . noble, pure and elevated," who would settle once and for all the "most delicate and intricate question" of "the human relation" ("The American Associationists," *United States Magazine and Democratic Review* 18 [February, 1846]: 146–47). But by the end Hester has largely overcome such "vain imaginings"; she has incorporated and transmuted them in a vision of continuity. In this larger sense her prophecy might be related to the statue of "Liberty" sculpted by Hiram Powers, upon whom Hawthorne modeled Kenyon, the artist-hero of *The Marble Faun.* Powers began work on the statue in Florence in 1848; by 1852 he was lamenting the misfortune of creating the "goodness of Liberty in this land of . . . anarchy," "but," he added, "as she is not likely to remain here very long it is to be hoped that she will not carry the infection [of European revolution] . . . with her to *America, where . . . her doctrine is received as gospel.*" Powers called the statue *America,* and Hawthorne, who urged Pierce to purchase it for the U.S. Capitol, approved the title, since "it embodies the ideas of youth, freedom, progress." The sculptor himself, he noted, was not only "a great artist" but "very American," and his work reflected this: "a female figure . . . vigorous, beautiful, planting its foot lightly

tler sex to the late sanguinary carnage at Paris, we are disposed to believe that such a revolting imputation proceeds from base calumniators, and is a libel upon woman.

By the intelligence, however, which we have lately received, the work of revolution is no longer confined to the Old World, nor to the masculine gender. The flag of independence has been hoisted, for the second time, on this side of the Atlantic; and a solemn league and covenant [as Cromwell termed the 1642 union of Scotland, Ireland, and England] has just been entered into by a Convention of Women at Seneca Falls.

[These radicals contend that the] great ordinances of God for the social regulation of man . . . are not to be endured if they cross the schemes of these reformers. . . . How often husbands abuse wives! . . . Dissolve, then, all single families. . . . Woman, too, is sometimes abused and oppressed. Therefore she must hold "Women's Rights Conventions" . . . openly defying the explicit commands of God. . . . In Europe most of the disorder in society has its origin in the domestic circle. . . . In the United States [on the contrary] the residence of the citizen is the image of order and peace. . . . As long as Americans shall preserve the severity of their moral conduct, they will preserve the democratic republic.

---

on a broken chain and pointing upward" (*French and Italian Notebooks*, *Works*, Centenary Edition, ed. Thomas Woodson [Columbus: Ohio State University Press, 1980], 14:436; Jean Fagan Yellin, "Caps and Chains: Hiram Powers' Statue of Liberty," *American Quarterly* 38 [1986]; 798–826). Emerson anticipates this figure in his vision of America's guardian "angel"–"sinless womanhood" in "Freedom's conquering cause" (*Indian Superstition* [1821], ed. Kenneth Cameron [Hanover, N.H.: Friends of Dartmouth Library, 1954], 11, 136–37). He elaborated upon it three decades later in his "Lecture Read before the Woman's Rights Convention, Boston, September 20, 1855": "Let us have the true woman . . . and no lawyer need be called in to write stipulations. . . . [She is] the best index of the coming hour. . . . All wisdoms Woman knows; though she . . . does not explain them" ("Woman," in *Works*, Riverside Edition, ed. J. E. Cabot [Boston: Houghton Mifflin, 1883], 11:355–56, 337, 340).

In a forthcoming study of gender in *The Scarlet Letter* and other fiction of the time, I consider this sociopolitical tradition in tandem with a much older legal-hermeneutical tradition that is also implicit in the A: the concept of the "feminine letter" in contradistinction (but ideally in complementary relation) to the "mail spirit"; and the long-established practice of branding the female offender with the *littera historia* of her transgression.

[But these women] seem to be really in earnest in their aim at revolution, and . . . evince confidence that [in the words of the *Marseillaise*] "the day of their deliverance is at hand."[6]

Surely Hawthorne means us to hear the strains of this American *Marseillaise,* this Cromwellian feminists' pact, in Hester's "stern and wild" irreverence (as indeed one of the novel's first reviewers pointed out and blamed him for embodying it in so strong a character). And surely too, Hawthorne's overall critique of Hester's radicalism—from her bitter sense of herself as "martyr" to her self-conscious manipulation of the townspeople and outright scorn for all "human institutions," "whatever priests or legislators had established" (259–60, 290)—registers the reaction against the rising European "carnage" and its "revolting" influence "on this side of the Atlantic."*

That reaction included all five major writers of F. O. Matthiessen's *American Renaissance*, in spite of their common devo-

*The connection noted earlier to Anne Hutchinson, or rather to Hawthorne's sketch of "Mrs. Hutchinson," is relevant here: first, in the defeminization of Hester (when a woman follows her own bent she "should be aware that she is relinquishing a part of the loveliness of her sex"); then, in the threat it poses to society, which Hawthorne associates with the "numerous . . . fair authors of our own day":

> there are portentous indications, changes gradually taking place in the habits and feelings of the gentle sex, which seem to threaten our posterity with many of those public women, whereof one was a burden too grievous for our fathers. . . . The evil is likely to be a growing one. As yet, the great body of American women are a domestic race; but when a continuance of ill-judged incitements shall have turned their hearts away from the fireside, there are obvious circumstances which will render female pens more numerous and more prolific than those of men;

and, most broadly (from Hawthorne's perspective), in the allusions to revolution through the link that Hawthorne recalls between Hutchinson and Sir Henry Vane, governor at the time the antinomian trials opened, who returned soon after to become an important figure under Cromwell: "In his mysterious eyes we may read a dark enthusiasm, akin to that of the woman whose cause he has espoused, combined with a shrewd worldly foresight, which tells him that her doctrines will be productive of change and tumult, the elements of his power and delight" (*Works*, Riverside Edition, ed. George Parsons Lathrop [Boston: Houghton Mifflin, 1883], 12: 217–26).

tion to "the possibilities of . . . democracy." Each of them responded in his own way, of course. Henry David Thoreau took the way of privacy and nature. "To read about things distant and sounding," he mused in his journals, "betrays us into slighting these which are then apparently near and small. . . . All summer and far into the fall I unconsciously went by the newspapers and the news, and now I find it was because the morning and the evening were full of news to me. . . . I attended not to affairs of Europe, but to my own affairs in Concord fields." This was not quietism. Thoreau could be fiercely partisan when the public threatened the sanctity of the individual. But insofar as the affairs of Europe meant "politics, revolutions, and wars," it was all "trivial." In *Walden* he elevates the trivial by transforming the battle between "the red republicans . . . and the black imperialists" into an epic war of the ants, or rather a mock-epic, framed in ironies ranging from the *Iliad* to the Book of Revelation. Its moral is suggested in journal entries of the time ("nothing new does ever happen in foreign parts, a French revolution not excepted") and in his response to visiting republican leaders, such as Italy's Giuseppe Mazzini and Hungary's Lajos Kossuth:

> It is a strange age of the world this, when empires, kingdoms, and republics come a-begging to our doors and utter their complaints at our elbows. I cannot take up the newspaper but I find that some wretched government or other, hard pushed and on its last legs, is interceding with me, the reader, to vote for it,—more importunate than an Italian beggar. . . . That excitement about Kossuth, consider how characteristic but superficial it was! . . . It is only another kind of dancing or of politics. . . . You can pass your hand under the largest mob, a nation in revolution even, and . . . not meet so much as a cobweb of support. They may not rest even by a point on eternal foundations. But an individual standing on truth you cannot pass your hand under. . . . So superficial these men [such as Kossuth and Mazzini] and their doings, it is life on a leaf or a chip which has nothing but air or water beneath.[7]

Walt Whitman was a political activist by comparison: barnburner delegate, Chartist sympathizer, admirer of Mazzini and Kossuth; but he found his way to a quintessentially liberal form of dissent. Through 1848 he was an outspoken advocate of revolution, denouncing all forms of oppression abroad, "modern" as well as "feudal," and going so far as to defend the French Republican Reign of Terror:

> Nature's force titanic here, the stronger and hardier for that repression—waiting terribly to break forth, revengeful . . . the tempest of massacres and blood. Yet who can wonder?
>
> Could we wish humanity different?
> Could we wish the people made of wood or stone?
> Or that there be no justice in destiny or time?

After 1849, however, when similar issues of injustice were raised in America itself—along with similar threats of revenge, carrying the prospect, Whitman feared, of "new governments, new laws, new social programs"—he steadily "recoiled." All that remains in *Leaves of Grass* of the Spirit of Forty-eight (when "Like lightning Europe le'pt forth") is

> . . . a Shape
> Vague as the night, draped interminably,
> head front and form, in scarlet folds
> Whose face and eyes none may see,
> Out of its robes only this . . . [*sic*] the red robes,
> lifted by the arm,
> One finger crook'd pointed high over the top, like
> the head of a snake appears.

Whitman consoled the "Foil'd European Revolutionaire" by recalling "that defeat [too] is great, / And that death and dismay are great"; and the moral he drew for "comeraderos" at home and abroad was "Educate, Educate,—it is the only true remedy for mobs, wild communistic theories, and red-republican ravings."[8]

Of all of Hawthorne's acquaintances only one, Margaret Fuller, continued to give her full support to the revolutionaries, and it has been argued persuasively that she figures not only in the ill-fated Zenobia of *The Blithedale Romance*, but, together with her allegedly illegitimate child (the gossip of Brahmin New England in 1849), in his portrait of the tormented radical, Hester Prynne. If so, it might be regarded as something of a Hawthornesque irony that Fuller returned from Europe "possessed," as she put it, "of a great history"–convinced of the importance of "social struggle" as against the "consolations of prophecy" ("The next revolution, here and elsewhere," she predicted, perhaps intending a critical allusion to 1776,* "will be an *un*compromising revolution")–and that she drowned within sight of the lifeboats grounded on the American shore.[9]

That was in 1850, which I take to be the centerpiece of the novel's authorial time frame. It was the year of the Compromise Resolutions, including the Fugitive Slave Act, and of *The Scarlet Letter.* Eighteen fifty-two marks the close of this period, with the return of Hawthorne's political fortune through the

*Fuller's relation to the American ideology is controversial. Certainly the European Forty-eight made her "more radical than ever": she proclaimed in her *Tribune* letters that socialism was "the inevitable sequence to the tendencies and wants of the era"; she told the "people of America" that they had yet to learn "the real meaning of the words, FRATERNITY, EQUALITY . . . [as well as] the needs of a true Democracy"; and some historians speculate that her lost manuscript was "a history of the Roman Republic told from a radical socialist's point of view" (Larry J. Reynolds, *European Revolutions and the American Literary Renaissance* [New Haven: Yale University Press, 1988], 56, 67, quoting Fuller). Still, in the absence of that manuscript, we can speak with certainty only of her published reports, which, as Bell Gale Chevigny observes, remain throughout grounded in the American symbology ("To the Edges of Ideology: Margaret Fuller's Centrifugal Evolution," *American Quarterly* 38, [1986]; 173–201). Her *Tribune* letter of May, 1848, is characteristic: "My friends talk of our country as the land of the future. It is so, but that spirit which makes it all it is of value in my eyes . . . is more alive here at present than in America" (*At Home and Abroad, or Things and Thoughts in America and Europe*, ed. A. B. Fuller [Boston: Crosby, Nichols, 1856], 326).

election to the presidency of his friend Franklin Pierce. Hawthorne did his share by writing the official campaign biography, in which he extols Pierce as "the statesman of practical sagacity—who loves his country *as it is,* and evolves good from things *as they exist*"—and he defends Pierce's support of the Fugitive Slave Act by comparing the abolitionists, indirectly, to Europe's "Red Republicans." The indirection suggests a political balancing act, somewhat like the Fugitive Slave Act itself: Hawthorne did not want to alienate those of Pierce's Young America supporters who persisted in identifying European insurrection with the claims of American expansionism. (Besides, Lajos Kossuth was then touring the United States, and, although Hawthorne himself felt "about as enthusiastic as a lump of frozen mud," he had to acknowledge the popularity of the Hungarian revolutionary leader.) Still, the comparatist implications in the Pierce biography are unmistakable. Hawthorne charges that, like the "terrorists of France," the abolitionists are hell-bent on chaos: they would tear "to pieces the Constitution" and sever "into distracted fragments that common country which Providence brought into one nation, through a continued miracle of almost two hundred years, from the first settlement of the American wilderness until the Revolution."[10]

As critics are coming increasingly to recognize, the Civil War provides the latent context of the American Renaissance. *Moby-Dick, The Narrative of Frederick Douglass,* and *Uncle Tom's Cabin* (as well as James Fenimore Cooper's apocalyptic last novel, *The Crater* [1849]) all deal more or less directly with loomings of national cataclysm. The visions of transcendent unity in *Walden, Leaves of Grass,* and Edgar Allan Poe's *Eureka* (1849) all depend on utopianism—utopian nostalgia in Thoreau's case, utopian futurism in Whitman's, dystopian metaphysics in Poe's—that circumvents or submerges actual divisions of the time. Considered together with the popular sentimental and gothic novels, these works provide a multivocal narrative of American liberal ideology during a crucial period of its formation. The special position of *The Scarlet Letter* in this narrative may be inferred from its centrist strategy: it employs sentimental themes and gothic techniques in order to mediate between utopian and dystopian resolutions, and, as we have seen, its return to cultural origins speaks to the threat of fragmentation while proposing the benefits of gradualism.

From that centrist perspective Hester's counsel (after the letter has done its office) seems a preview of Hawthorne's answer to the abolitionists. Slavery, he explains in the Pierce biography, is "one of those evils which divine Providence does not leave to be remedied by human contrivances, but which, in its own good time, by some means impossible to be anticipated, but of the simplest and easiest operation, when all its uses shall have been fulfilled, it causes to vanish like a dream."[11] Only the security of commonplace could allow for this daring inversion in logic, whereby slavery is represented symbolically, as part of the "continued miracle" of America's progress. Like the scarlet letter, Hawthorne's argument has the power of a long-preserved cultural artifact.

But of course the two artifacts are different in kind. The argument in the biography reflects a certain tactic of the culture; its power derives from a system of ideas connecting racism and progress. The power of the scarlet letter derives from its capacities for mediation. It reveals the variety of tactics available to the culture at a certain historical moment. And, as I have noted, antebellum culture was particularly volatile—in the sense now not of transition, but of consolidation: volatility redirected into channels of social growth. It was a culture feeding on change, nourished by technological innovation, urbanization, commercial growth, territorial expansion, shifts of power centers, and waves of immigration, and, as a symptom of its increasing confidence, accommodating itself to new conditions by moving toward a resolution by violence of its major internal conflict. To call Hawthorne's racism a cultural tactic is not to excuse it, but to distinguish the biography from the novel. Considered as part of an intracultural debate, his response to the Fugitive Slave Act differs dramatically from that of abolitionists like Emerson and Stowe. As Henry James pointed out,

> Hawthorne was a Democrat, and apparently a zealous one; even in his later years, after the Whigs had vivified their principles by the tion of the Republican platform, and by taking up an honest attitude on the question of slavery, his political faith never wavered. His Democratic sympathies were eminently natural, and there would have been an incongruity in his belonging to the other party.[12]

But incongruity is not contradiction, and, if we step outside the boundaries of intracultural debate, the difference between Hawthorne's "natural" Democratic allegiances and the "vivified" Whig platform he opposed reflects something else entirely: a series of no-longer-avoidable conflicts within a system whose principles and prejudices (including racism and American exceptionalism) were shared by virtually all parties and, though not equally, by Whigs and Democrats alike. *The Life of Pierce* advances what turned out to be an inadequate mode of resolving a social crisis. *The Scarlet Letter* expresses a particular culture's mode of resolving crisis. It is not that the novel transcends propaganda. It is that its imaginative forms incorporate the complexity of beliefs implicit in any single-minded doctrine we commonly associate with propaganda. Hawthorne's biography is based on partisan issues; it takes a certain stand within an enclosed set of options and advances a particular course of action out of several then available to the culture. His novel explores various options available within a set of interlinked forms of thought and expression. Where *The Life of Pierce* presents a certain choice, *The Scarlet Letter* represents a metaphysics of choosing. It advocates not a particular course of action but a worldview within which that course of action makes sense and takes effect.

We might call the novel thick propaganda. Its range of possibilities includes most forms of resolution generated by the antebellum North. To repeat the logic of Hester's vision (insofar as it prefigures the Pierce biography), injustice is to be removed by some "divine operation," which, however, has not yet done its office. This representation of conflict as ambiguity, and of ambiguity as an absence-to-be (an injustice to be eliminated), is not substantially different from the Liberian solution (deportation of African Americans) endorsed by Harriet Beecher Stowe and enacted in the happy ending to *Uncle Tom's Cabin* by her mulatto hero, George Harris. Nor is it different in substance from the expansionist argument that to repeal the Fugitive Slave Act would renew the errand—would inspire the "children of the Puritans," as John Greenleaf Whittier wrote (echoing Dimmesdale's prophecy), to cross "the prairie as of old / The pilgrims crossed the sea" and thereby ("Upbearing like the Ark of old, / The Bible in our van") hasten "Freedom's holy Pentecost." Nor again is Hawthorne's solution different in substance from that proposed a decade later by those who believed *they* were the divine operation, providence incarnate, moving irresistibly toward the Armageddon of the Republic. In his debates with Douglas, Lincoln effectually reversed Hawthorne's argument—it was the anti-abolitionists, he charged, who were fragmenting the Union and subverting the fathers' legacy—and in his Second Inaugural Address (1865), reviewing the causes of the Civil War, he described American slavery as "one of those offences which, in the providence of God, must needs come, but which, having continued through His appointed time, He now wills to remove."[13]

The difference between Lincoln's counsel for reconciliation and Hester's for patience is the turn of a certain circular symbolic logic. The Northern rhetoric of the Civil War represents negation as affirmation—the destined union made manifest in violence. Hawthorne's rhetoric builds on affirmation by negation—manifest inaction justified by national destiny. From this perspective it is worth recalling the enormous force of the negative imperative in *The Scarlet Letter.* Negation is far more than a form of moral, political, and aesthetic control. It is the very ground of Hawthorne's strategy of process as closure: the antidialectics of ambiguity and irony through which he absorbs and refashions the radical energies of history. "The scarlet letter had not done its office": negation leads us forward toward that deeper significance that Hawthorne promises at the start—that comprehensive "deep meaning . . . most worthy of interpretation" (145–46)—precisely by evoking the fear of process run amok; the prospect (which indeed was to be actualized in 1852 as *Pierre; or, The Ambiguities*) of history becoming conflicting stories of disruptions; multiple meanings dissolving into irreconcilability; ironic reversals tending not so much downwards, toward the tragic, as nowhere, toward the absurd; pluralism fragmenting into sheer diversity; gaps, absences, and omissions raised to an antistructural "demon Principle": "Silence is the only Voice of our God."[14]

It is the overt purpose of Hawthorne's negations to preclude that eventuality. But his strategy goes further than that. It almost may be said to take on a counterdynamic of its own, as though in opposite and equal reaction to the fear of uncontrolled process. Negation gathers such momentum in the course of the novel that it threatens the very process it was designed to guide. Not doing its office almost comes to define the function of the symbol. When, after "seven miserable years," Hester at last finds the strength to discard the A, it takes all of Hawthorne's resources (providence, Pearl, Dimmesdale, and nature itself) to have her restore it against her will. And even so the restoration serves at first to highlight the letter's negative effects. As she awaits her moment of flight with Dimmesdale, Hester stands alone in the marketplace with a "frozen calmness," her face a death mask, and because of that, with all the radical vitality for which we have come to admire her:

> after sustaining the gaze of the multitude through seven miserable years as a necessity, a penance, and something which it was a stern religion to endure, she now, for one last time more, encountered it freely and voluntarily, in order to convert what had so long been agony into a kind of triumph. "Look your last on the scarlet-letter and its wearer!"—the people's victim and life-long bond-slave, as they fancied her, might say to them. "Yet a little while, and she will be beyond your reach! A few hours longer, and the deep, mysterious ocean will quench and hide for ever the symbol which ye have caused to burn upon her bosom!" (313–14)

That is why Hawthorne must bring her back, and, more than that, must force her to resume the A "freely and voluntarily," of her own free will. It is as though under pressure of her resistance the letter were slipping out of his grasp, losing its efficacy as an agent of reconciliation. In terms of what I called the novel's latent context, the impending Civil War, the antinomies in this passage ("people" and "victim," "freely" and "bond-slave") assume an explosive force, an almost irrepressible tendency toward confrontation, which endangers process and closure alike. That tendency may be seen as the political aftereffect of the rhetoric of liberty, in which "slavery" served ambiguously, as Bernard Bailyn has shown, to denote all forms of bondage, private or public, civil or political, including (for Margaret Fuller and other feminists) the bond slavery of women to men. More directly, it is the rhetorical counterpart of what Edmund Morgan, describing the ironies of antebellum politics, termed "American freedom / American slavery."[15] It is a testament to Hawthorne's sensitivity to those rhetorical-political tensions that he allowed the danger to surface, that indeed he played it out almost to the point of no return. It is a testament to the resilience of the ideology it drew upon that nonetheless he could resume process, impose closure, and, as it were, rescue the symbol from the ocean's depths, by simply, sweepingly, *assuming* an interpretive consensus.

For the silence surrounding Hester's final conversion to the letter is clearly deliberate on Hawthorne's part. Like the silence that precedes Dimmesdale's decision to confess, it mystifies Hester's choice by forcing us to represent it through the act of interpretation. Having given us ample directives about how to understand the ambiguous ways in which the letter had not done its office and having set out the ironies that thread the pattern of American consensus from 1649 to 1849, Hawthorne now depends on us to recognize—freely and voluntarily, for his method depends on his seeming not to impose meaning—the need for Hester's return. In effect, he invites us to participate in a free enterprise democracy of symbol making. Its cultural model is the ambiguity universalized in the Declaration of Independence: "*We* hold these truths to be *self*-evident" (my emphasis). The silent problematic of "we" may be inferred from Pip's revelation of the plural meanings of the doubloon—"I look, you look, he looks, we look, ye look, they look"—especially if we remember, as Pip seems not to, that *this* doubloon has a single-minded purpose and that his pluralist grammatical declension masks a social hierarchy, *descending* from the captain's "I" to the ship-stokers' "they." The silenced problematic of "self-evident" may be inferred from the quasi-voluntaristic terms of Ahab's covenant: "I do not order ye; ye will it."[16]

Hawthorne, too, may be said to elicit these problematics, but, unlike Melville, he does so in order to guide us toward accommodation. When, in the most carefully prepared-for reversal in classic American literature, Hester herself imposes the symbol; she signals her recognition that what had seemed a basic problem—basic enough to have made her want to overturn society—is really a question of point of view; and Hawthorne so veils this epiphany that our multiple perspectives enact the same ideal of liberal community, *e pluribus unum, ex unum plures*, that his novel celebrates and represents.

It is an oblique mode of celebration, and, as I have been arguing, all the more persuasive for its obliquity. Pierre Macherey argues that gaps and silences in narrative structure—the sorts of indirection in which Hawthorne specializes—demarcate the limits of ideology. According to Macherey, they are symptoms of fissures in the culture, the contradictions that the system can neither absorb nor wholly exclude.[17] His theory seems especially pertinent to classic American literature, which abounds in strategies of process through hiatus, and to Hawthorne's work in particular. It is pertinent first of all because it conspicuously does *not* apply to the narrative gap that precedes Hester's return. Hawthorne makes that silence reverberate with all the voices of cultural authority; he transforms the gap into an ideological bridge (spanning three centuries now) between character, author, and reader. When midway through the novel we accept Hawthorne's judgment that the scarlet letter had not done its office, we acquiesce to the narrative in a willing suspension of disbelief; but at the end when we ourselves require the letter to be imposed, inventing reasons (all of them necessarily indirect and ironical) or synthesizing the views of others (each of them necessarily incomplete and ambiguous), we invest our very will to suspend disbelief in a joint-stock company of pluralist interpretation. It is a leap of cultural faith for which the entire novel has been our preparation.

What I would suggest is the ideological *power* of gaps and silences. As Norman Mailer writes in *The Armies of the Night: History as a Novel, The Novel as History* (1968): "From gap to gain is very American." In the mid-nineteenth century, that fictive-factual quality found its main expression in the rhetoric of expansion, opportunity, speculation, and enterprise; the symbiosis between verbal and territorial appropriation inherent in the appeal to "open country," "virgin land," "empty continent," "unmapped future"; the Thoreauvian interior "white on the chart" of the self; the Emersonian "I" that *becomes all* by *being nothing*. Lansford Hastings's *Emigrant's Guide to Oregon and California*, perhaps the most consulted handbook of its kind, equates the unbounded territories ahead with "the unbounded happiness . . . of civilized and enlightened man." "The expansive future is our arena, and for our history," declared John O'Sullivan in an essay on "The Great Nation of Futurity." "We are entering on its untrodden space. . . . The far-reaching, the boundless future will be the era of American greatness." "By persisting to read or to think," writes Emerson in "Experience," thinking of the visionary West of the imagination,

> this region gives further sign of itself . . . in sudden discoveries of its profound beauty . . . as if the clouds that covered it parted at intervals, and showed the approaching traveller the inland mountains with the tranquil eternal meadows spread at their base. But every insight is felt as initial, and promises a sequel. I do not make it; I arrive there, and behold what was there already, I make![18]

The link I am suggesting between transcendentalism and expansionism is a matter not just of a common rhetoric but of cultural symbology—that is, a matter of rhetoric as the expression of a common vision and mode of identity. Part of the long foreground to the interior West of "Experience" is the frontier movement (as Emerson understood it) from New England to the Pacific. The Puritans, he explained, had developed a

> wonderful personal independence. . . . Later this strength appears in the solitudes of the West, where man is made a hero by the varied emergencies of his lonely farm, and neighborhoods must combine against the Indians, or the horse-thieves, or the river rowdies, by organizing themselves into committees of vigilance. . . . [Hence the "open, onward-moving" character of frontiersmen, who] can find a way out of any peril. This rough and ready force becomes them, and makes them fit citizens and civilizers.

This heroic, civilizing spirit is not fundamentally different from that in which John O'Sullivan in 1845 consecrated the term "manifest destiny" in an editorial supporting the annexation of Texas:

> it may perhaps be required of us as a necessary condition of the freedom of our institutions, that we must live on for ever in a state of unpausing struggle and excitement . . . [for it is] our manifest destiny to overspread the continent allotted by Providence for [our] free development. . . . [I]ndeed there is a great deal of Annexation *yet to take place.*

Later that year, commemorating the death of Andrew Jackson, Bancroft predicted that the "next great office to be performed by America, is the taking possession of the wilderness." And a year later, in 1846, the explorer-pioneer-politician William Gilpin defined that "great office" in terms that may be said to foreshadow the prophecies of Dimmesdale and Hester. It was "the *untransacted* destiny of the American people," Gilpin told Congress, "to subdue the continent . . . [and] unite the world in one social family"—a phrase that Charles Dana recalled in *The Garden of the World: or, The Great West* (1856) and extended to include the millennium: "The *Land of Promise,* and the *Canaan* of our time . . . shall go on conquering and to conquer, until the whole earth shall resound with its fame and glory."[19]

These vacancies of time and space were constructed so that the facts they displaced could be filled by a certain symbolic outlook.* And the act of displacement had a double function, teleological and processual. The teleology served to white out the actual course of emptying a continent. For all narrative and

*One aspect of this outlook is the office of "American English," as developed from Noah Webster through Horace Bushnell and epitomized, as Michael P. Kramer has shown, in Whitman's vision of a New World "lexicon as broad and inclusive . . . as the American territories, as varied as the occupations of its inhabitants, [and] as extensive as nature and history and human experience" (*Imagining Language in America: From the Revolution to the Civil War* [Princeton, N.J.: Princeton University Press, 1990], 203). The English language, Whitman believed, was "America's Mightiest Inheritance"—not because of its mighty legacy (Geoffrey Chaucer, William Shakespeare, and William Wordsworth) but, on the contrary, because it was the language of the future, of the still unarticulated and unnamed. Alfred Lord Tennyson's English was the voice of stasis, closure, and the past; American English was "the true broad fluid language of democracy":

explanatory purposes, including the narratives of region and nation, it covered up the history of the indigenous peoples, while at the same time keeping the constructed identity of regions and nation open-ended, "untransacted," "uncharted"—an office, as it were, on an errand. The second function of displacement concerned the gradual westward movement. I refer to the threat posed by expansionism in a liberal culture: the clash of multiple interests; competing errands; and states, territories, and regions in collision. As Thomas Jefferson put it on April 13, 1820 (seventeen years after he engineered the Louisiana Purchase and launched the Lewis and Clark expedition):

> The Missouri question aroused and filled me with alarm. The old schism of federal and republican threatened nothing, because it existed in every State, and united them together by the fraternalism of the party. But the coincidence of a marked principle, moral and political, with a geographical line, once conceived, I feared would never more be obliterated from the mind; that it would be recurring on every occasion and renewing irritations; until it would kindle such mutual and mortal hatred, as to render separation preferable to eternal discord.[20]

> Language . . . of all who aspire,
> Language of growth . . .
> Language to well-nigh express the inexpressible,
> Language for the modern, language of America.

("Poem of Many in One," in *Leaves of Grass* [1856; reprint, n.p.: Norwood Press, 1976], 191)

And of course it was language in process, "yet to be acclimated here." "The blank," writes Whitman, which is "left by words wanted"—the semantic gap that registers our limitations—also signifies the democratic vistas ahead: "When time comes to represent any thing or state of things, the words will surely follow"; then "the American mind shall boldly penetrate to the interiors of all," and Americans, accordingly, will emerge as "the most perfect users of words," "the most fluent and melodious voiced people in the world" (America's Mightiest Inheritance" [1856], in *New York Dissected: A Sheaf of Recently Discovered Newspaper Articles by the Author of "Leaves of Grass,"* ed. Emory Holloway and Ralph Adiamari [New York: R. R. Wilson, 1936], 49–63; "Our Language and Literature" [1856], in *Daybooks and Notebooks*, ed. William White [New York: New York University Press, 1978], 3: 732, 745–46, 810–11).

From either perspective, processual or teleological, the vacancies of Jacksonian America served to make the territory anew—negatively, as "wilderness," positively as "Nature"—in order to shape the mind of its invaders in accordance with that ideological newness. The West was the scene of imperial rhetoric throughout the Americas, from the Canadian bush country to the Spanish-American El Dorado, but only in the United States did the dominant culture find a rhetoric commensurate with territorial prospects: a symbology of wonder that could reconstitute the new inhabitants (and successive waves of immigrants after them) as a tabula rasa to be imprinted with images of America ("Adamic," "innocent") and typed forth as "representative Americans."[21] The correspondences here between nature, the mind, spiritual rebirth, and national mission build directly on the language of errand. They create a sort of alchemical *nihilum ex verbo*, a perpetual gap between words and facts through which words are transmuted into a prophetic evidence and facts refined into symbols in transition, not unlike the scarlet letter.

This is the imperial office of the American rhetoric of process.* Its ironies of time and space are encapsulated, with "a cer-

*Its spiritual dimension, what we might call the office of representative selfhood, can be traced from Emerson's "American Scholar," in which personal transcendence finds both its objective correlative and its moral imperative in the "continent" at large—the "Americanness" of the gap-to-be-bridged in 1837 between twenty-six states and the projected continental "nation of men"); and from that "*extra-vagant*" summons to "re-commencement" it may be traced through Henry James's vision of expanding consciousness, as expressed by Isabel Archer, beginning her travels with "the world all before" her: "Nothing that belongs to me is any measure of me; everything's on the contrary a limit, a barrier, and a perfectly arbitrary one" (Emerson, *Essays and Lectures*, ed. Joel Porte [New York: Library of America, 1983], 53, 71; Thoreau, *Walden; or Life in the Woods*, in *A Week on the Concord and Merrimack Rivers, Walden, The Maine Woods, Cape Cod*, ed. Robert F. Sayre [New York: Library of America, 1985], 580; James, *The Portrait of a Lady*, in *Novels, 1881–1886*, ed. William T. Stafford [New York: Library of America, 1985], 798, 398).

By the late nineteenth century this rhetoric of process had come openly to serve the office of imperialism—though still as counterpart to an America "where no man is supposed to be under any limitation, except the limitations

tain deep, sad undertone of pathos" (233), in Dimmesdale's forecast of the continental wilderness to be planted. At mid-century they served a variety of other purposes as well—most conspicuously, perhaps, that of "Union through Compromise." I refer to the antebellum resolutions enacted under "the great triumvirate" (John C. Calhoun, Henry Clay, and Daniel Webster), in which North and South agreed to mutual concessions, accommodating the interests of both regions. "The Constitution of the United States," explained Webster, speaking for the North, "consists in a series of mutual agreements or compromises." To accede, then, to *certain* demands of Southern slaveholders, such as the Fugitive Slave Act, was precisely the sort of reciprocity that the founders intended. In 1850 as in 1789, compromise was "the one rock forever, as solid as the granite of [our] hills, for the Union to repose on." It showed all the various "States . . . revolving in separate spheres, and yet mutually bound one with another." "The Propositions to Compromise," declared Senator Clay of Kentucky, were the "sacred rules" by which "this country has run from the adoption of the Constitution down to the present" and the basis for its unparalleled success, economically, militarily, politically, and morally, beyond that of any other "nation upon which the sun of Heav-

---

of character and the mind" (Woodrow Wilson, *The New Freedom* [New York: Doubleday, 1913], 14). At mid-century it served primarily for "internal" purposes (notably, expansion and consolidation), as the contrast between Pearl and Isabel Archer suggests. Ever since Harry Levin's *The Power of Blackness: Hawthorne, Poe, Melville* ([New York: Knopf, 1958], 242), critics have spoken of the adult Pearl as a prefiguration of James's American abroad. I would add to this suggestive connection the contextual implications of the dramatic change involved in character-conception and plot development and the rhetorical continuities that circumscribe that change—both within the novels, as in the symbology of Old World versus New, and in the culture at large, as in the rhetoric of annexation that links Thomas Jefferson's advocacy of the Louisiana Purchase (1803), through Franklin Pierce's rationale for the Mexican War (1846–48) to Theodore Roosevelt's claims for "imperial democracy" at the turn of our century.

en has shone." In short, as the newspapers of the day put it, to compromise was "to defend the Constitution inviolate and to MAINTAIN THE UNION."[22]

This concept of consensus through concession had behind it the authority of the growth of American democracy. As both Northern and Southern legislators pointed out, it was not just that "the Constitution [itself] was the compromise"—the nation's "binding compromise . . . faithfully kept by every congress from 1789 to 1850"—but that the Constitution had inaugurated a continuing process of economic, political, and territorial acts of concession. Not even William Seward, Webster's leading opponent, challenged that processual "vindication of American institutions." Indeed, Seward attacked the Fugitive Slave Act as a "novelty" that countermanded "the compromising expedient [concerning slavery] of the Constitution." His famous dictum that "there is a higher law than the Constitution" was intended to universalize (not challenge) the terms of Constitutional rule. The higher law, as Seward expounded it, was manifest in the "sublime and benevolent" decisions of the founders as they "deliberated . . . the institutions we enjoy." On that basis Bushnell defended abolition pragmatically as "The Doctrine of Loyalty":

> there was a Constitution here, if we may so speak, before the Constitution, a nation before the defined Articles of nationality. It required, in fact, as good and high loyalty to fight the Providential nation out into independence, as it now does to defend it. Nay, it required more loyalty to make the Constitution, than it ever can to keep it. It was that old providential Constitution, too, prior to the Constitution . . . that gave the Convention itself a right to say by what kind of vote the Constitution should be binding; for, if the body had no right, stood in no providential order, then the vote prescribed never had or can have any binding force.

On that basis, too, in his decisive anti-abolitionist oration of March 7—which, its publisher tells us, "in consideration of the manner in which it was received throughout the country, has been entitled a speech for 'the Constitution and the Union'—Webster defined compromise as the "common center" around which the Republic's multiple interests were "now revolving in harmony."[23]

It is pertinent that in 1850 the word "compromise" did not carry the primarily pejorative meaning it does today: "a committal to something derogatory"; "to expose to suspicion, or discredit or mischief"; "to make a shameful or disreputable concession." For the legislative majority who voted in the Compromise Resolutions, the term meant above all (according to Noah Webster's standard *American Dictionary*) "to bind by mutual agreement," where the principles of binding had the doubled force of contract and covenant: "an amicable agreement between parties in controversy to settle their differences, by mutual concessions"; "a mutual promise"; "an engagement to refer matters in dispute to the decision of arbitrators"; "to adjust and settle"; "to pledge by some act or declaration"; and "see *Promise*." The weak point lay in the vagueness of "promise," especially under what turned out to be the diverse pressures to concede: "pledge" versus "arbitration" versus "declaration" versus "agreement." By the close of the Jacksonian period, vagueness had taken the form of ambiguity. It had always been a subsidiary possibility that "compromise" *could* mean "to put to hazard." But in the literature at mid-century that meaning takes on a sudden prominence. To all appearances the increasing dysfunctions of "amicable agreements" from Massachusetts to Kansas—and from the Missouri Compromise of 1820 (which established slavery in Missouri while prohibiting it in the Nebraska Territory) to the various mid-century compromises over Southwest territories—were affecting the course of "American English." If so, it is crucial to Hawthorne's achievement that the apotheosis of compromise—rhetorically, in Webster's great orations from 1848 to 1850 and, politically, as the "National Platform" that swept Pierce into office in 1852—came at the moment when the term was undergoing a decisive change.[24]

Between 1848 and 1852 the unbound, open-ended ambiguity that the term "hazard" had brought into play endowed the primary meaning of "compromise" with the power of what Freud called the antithetical sense of primal words. "Compromise: *consent* reached by *mutual concession*"—all the volatile doubleness that had been explicit in the revolutionary keyword "independent" (isolated versus fully developed) and implicit in the ubiquitous Jacksonian "self" prefix (self-made versus self-serving versus self-reliant versus self-centered) exploded in antebellum America in the struggle between the party for union and the party against concession. Both parties laid claim to consent, of course, as the touchstone of liberal consensus. They were divided mainly on pragmatics—the scope of consent, the nature of consensus—but it was now a pragmatism *at hazard*, charged with apocalyptic import. Daniel Webster's concession to the South, according to Emerson, "was the darkest passage in [our] history," a "disastrous defection (on the miserable cry of Union)," from "the principles of culture and progress." For his part Webster pointed to the specter of European revolution, fratricide, terror, and collapse, and, against all this, speaking "not as a Massachusetts man, nor as a northern man, but as an American," he invoked the spirit of compromise embodied from its Puritan origins in the American city on a hill. With "the eyes of all Christendom upon us," he pleaded—with the "whole world . . . looking towards us with extreme anxiety"—"let our comprehension be as broad as our country" and "our aspirations as high": let us make visible at last the "certain destiny . . . that belongs to us."[25]

From the revolutions of 1848 through the election of Franklin Pierce, this rhetoric of compromise occupied the center of a debate whose extremes were pro-slavery constitutionalism and pro-constitutional abolitionism. I refer here to the debate within the dominant culture, but it is astonishing how few voices broke the parameters of liberal discourse in what elsewhere (to recall the phrases of *The Scarlet Letter*) was a time of "radical speculation," "an age in which the human intellect, newly emancipated, had taken a more active and wider range than for many centuries before." This holds true even for the abolitionist Constitution burner William Lloyd Garrison, even for the anti-Garrisonian abolitionist Frederick Douglass, and certainly for such mainstream Liberianists as Sarah Hale and Harriet Beecher Stowe. As for Hawthorne, he scarcely wavered in his centrist convictions. In the Pierce biography he recalled "The Compromise" as a triumphant "test" of "the reverence of the people for the Constitution, and their attachment to the Union," and, as late as 1858, he said of a statue of Webster, "symbolizing him as the preserver of the Union, . . . I never saw such . . . massive strength . . . [and] deep, pervading energy. . . . He looks really like a pillar of the state . . . very grand, very Webster . . . he is in the act of meeting a great crisis, and yet with the warmth of a great heart glowing through it."[26] But by then the crisis of industrial capitalism was calling for new sources of strength. After 1852, with Webster's death and the struggle for the Free states, the central cultural symbols shifted steadily to embrace the armies of the North, wielding God's terrible swift sword to cut the gordian knot of consent/concession.

Not the ends but the means had changed. Compromise, "to bind by mutual agreement," had failed to provide either the mechanism for binding or the metaphors for agreement, and with due alacrity the leaders of the dominant culture had moved to preserve the Union against the hazards of ambiguity. In 1853 Sarah Hale, a leading woman of letters and advocate of abolition (with deportation), made it a credo of Godey's *Ladies Magazine*, the most popular journal of the time, to supplement male mutual agreements with the "uncompromising spirituality" of the domestic sphere. "'Constitutions' and 'compromises' are the appropriate work of men," she explained, but "women are conservators of moral power"; and while "individual liberty [is] secured by constitutional laws," "WOMAN is God's appointed agent of *morality* . . . destined to the most spiritual offices . . . intended as the teacher and the inspirer" not of compromise but of "absolute and spiritual law." A year later that incipiently divisive ambiguity invaded the sphere of political power as well. The debates over the Kansas-Nebraska Bill involved, on one side, the federal Committee on Territories, which invoked the 1820 Missouri Compromise as the "way to progress and popular sovereignty," and, on the other side, the Independent Democrats, who argued that to compromise meant "a gross violation of a sacred pledge," a "desecration of our covenant with destiny." In 1858, some four months before Hawthorne's encomium to Webster, Lincoln set out the new rhetoric of consent in a Senate campaign speech that not only recombined "popular sovereignty" with "covenant" and "pledge" but also actually appropriated the Southern imagery of fragmentation for the Yankee cause: "I do not expect the house to *fall*—but I *do* expect it will cease to be divided. It will become *all* one thing, or *all* the other." The next year Emerson displayed the recuperative powers of that revision in his tribute to John Brown.* Far from being a threat to consensus, "the hero of Harper's Ferry," he said, was the

*The parameters of revision—and, ipso facto, the boundaries of vision—are suggested in the parallels between the strategies of consensus after the Revolution and those at the end of the Civil War. In 1788 James Madison sought to calm the anti-Federalists by invoking the ambiguities of consensus at the recent Constitutional Convention: "neither side would entirely yield to the other, and consequently . . . the struggle could be terminated only by compromise"—a compromise that made manifest (once again) "that Almighty hand which has been so frequently and signally extended to our relief in the critical stages of the revolution" (Federalist 37, in *Federalist Papers*, ed. Max Beloff [London: Basil Blackwell, 1987], 180–81). Some eighty years later Lincoln sought to reconcile anti-Unionists by explaining the Civil War as a broken compromise and reunion as a set of mutual agreements to be divinely restored: "To strengthen, perpetuate, and extend their interest was the object for which the [Southern] insurgents would rend the Union, even by war; while the government [in 1861] claimed no right to do more than to restrict the territorial enlargement of it. . . . The prayers of both [sides] could not be answered; that of neither has been answered fully. The Almighty has His own purposes"—purposes that for Lincoln as for Madison had been

> representative of the American Republic. . . . He joins that perfect Puritan faith which brought his fifth ancestor to Plymouth Rock, with his grandfather's ardor in the Revolution. He believes in two articles—two instruments shall I say?—the Golden Rule and the Declaration of Independence.[27]

"Instruments" was the better word. It is a nice irony of our literary history that Hawthorne's absolutist Concord neighbors, Emerson and Thoreau, managed to span the spectrum of response, whereas skeptical, many-faceted Hawthorne remained ideologically fixated, like some Ahab of compromise. I do not think we can say that his incapacity to accept the change ruined his career, as it did Pierce's and Webster's. But to some extent at least it drained him of crucial intellectual and moral resources. On some level it accounts for the increasing tendency of his fiction to expose (rather than reconcile) ideological contradictions. For the fact is that of all his novels it is only about *The Scarlet Letter* that we can say, as Henry James did *in praise of* Hawthorne's art, that "the reader must look for his local and national qualities between the lines of his writing and in the *indirect* testimony of his tone, his accent, his temper, of his very omissions and suppressions." Consider the difference in this respect between Hester's return on the one hand and on the other Holgrave's strained conversion, Coverdale's problematic confession, or, most pointedly, the much-disputed homecoming of Hilda, that other wandering daughter of the Puritans.* In his European letters and journals, Hawthorne often hints at

inscribed (*through* conflict) by an "Almighty hand . . . frequently and signally extended to our relief" (Second Inaugural Address, 1865, in *Works*, ed. Roy P. Balser [New Brunswick, N.J.: Rutgers University Press, 1953], 8: 333).

*In the case of *The Marble Faun*, readers from the start demanded explanations for the gaps between process and closure, as Hawthorne acidly notes in the novel's conclusion (where he insists instead on his technique of indirectness). In the case of the earlier novels, critics have sought to convert narrative weaknesses into authorial strengths by assuming that Hawthorne *intended* the weaknesses—planted these as clues by which he meant for us to demystify cultural myths. Thus, in *The House of the Seven Gables* the sudden transmu-

the cause of his failing strategies of omission. He is most explicit in the preface to his last book, *Our Old Home,* which appropriately he dedicated to his old friend Franklin Pierce:

The Present, the Immediate, the Actual, has proved too potent for me. It takes away not only my scanty faculty, but even my desire for imaginative composition, and leaves me sadly content to scatter a thousand peaceful fantasies upon the hurricane that is sweeping us all along with it, possibly, into a Limbo where our nation and its polity may be as literally the fragments of a shattered dream as my unwritten Romance.[28]

This was 1863, at the height of the war, and it is not hard to understand Hawthorne's bewilderment and dismay. Henry James's views are pertinent in this respect:

Our hero was an American of the earlier and simpler type—the type of which it is doubtless premature to say that it has wholly passed away, but of which it may at least be said that the circumstances that produced it have been greatly modified. The generation to which he belonged, that generation which grew up with the century, witnessed during a period of fifty years the immense, uninterrupted material development of the young Republic; and when one thinks of the scale on which it took place . . . there seems to be little room for surprise that it should have implanted a kind of superstitious faith in the grandeur of the country. . . . This faith was a simple and uncritical one, enlivened with an element of genial optimism, in the light of which it appeared that the great American state was not as other human institutions are, that a special Providence watched over it. . . .

The brightness of [this] outlook . . . was not made greater by the explosion of the Civil War in the spring of 1861. These months, and the three years that followed them, were not a cheerful time for any persons but army-contractors; but over Hawthorne the war-cloud appears to have dropped a permanent shadow. The whole affair was

---

tation of the curse of private property (as by Adam Smith's invisible hand of God) into the blessings of suburban mobility is interpreted, along with Holgrave's conversion, as a subversive strategy on Hawthorne's part, designed to undermine the narrator so as to direct his readers to "a troublesome encounter in which our presuppositions are altered" (Brook Thomas, "*The House of the Seven Gables:* Reading the Romance of America," *PMLA* 93 [1978]: 208).

a bitter disappointment to him, and a fatal blow to that happy faith in the uninterruptedness of American prosperity which I have spoken of as the religion of the old-fashioned American.

If we disregard James's personal condescension (a symptom of authorial anxiety) and his blindness to the *complexities* of "the young Republic" (a symptom of his debt to certain cultural myths, including the typology of national progress), this description is not only accurate but poignant. In 1860 Hawthorne had returned to an America where (he professed to believe) there was "no shadow, no antiquity, no mystery, no picturesque and gloomy wrong, nor anything but a commonplace prosperity, in broad and simple daylight." Two years later he confessed in an essay "Chiefly About War-Matters": "the general heart-quake of the country long ago knocked at my cottage-door, and compelled me, reluctantly, to suspend the contemplation of certain fantasies." We might well see in this image (as in that limbo of shattered dreams) an unconscious inversion of Hester's return. But we should also keep in mind the hurricanes of the actual which a decade earlier had *not* disturbed Hawthorne's fantasies: Southern slavery; Native American genocide; the Mexican War (through which General Pierce became a national hero); expansionist demands by men like Pierce for war against Cuba and Latin America; pervasive ethnic and religious discrimination; child labor in Northern mill towns; the grievances listed by the Seneca Falls Convention; and the manifold abuses documented in the petitions circulated by New England's abolitionist sewing circles.[29]

Hawthorne was aware in 1850 of those present and pressing evils. Some of them earlier had found their way into his short stories; some are actually recorded in the Pierce biography; others may be said to underlie the discontents that Hester, in her sewing circle of one, embroiders into her scarlet letter; still others are implicit in her confrontation with the immigrant "bond-servant" at Governor Bellingham's mansion, "a free-born

Englishman, but now a seven years' slave" (206); and others again may be discerned in the "sorrows and perplexities" that the townspeople bring to Hester after her return, "demanding why they were so wretched, and what the remedy!" No American writer felt more detached from party politics than Hawthorne did; few were more engaged in the affairs of political office; and none was so deeply learned in American political history. There is no surprise in this claim. Hawthorne sought to rise above politics not by escaping history, but by representing it ironically. To that end, in "The Custom-House" introduction he exposes the miasma of mid-nineteenth-century patronage and, in the novel proper, the excesses of partisanship.

The hiatus between introduction and story is the ideological link between Hawthorne and Hester. Her reconciliation at the end is the link in turn between the novel and the biography: first, in the image that Hester may be said to project of Hawthorne's return to the patronage system; then, in the biographical image of Pierce as the great reconciler; and, finally, in Hawthorne's implied contrast between process in the New World and upheaval in the Old. Revolutionary Europe, in this view, was political in the narrow sectarian, exclusivist meaning of ideology. The United States transcended ideology, so defined, for the same reason that the concept of America transcended politics: because, as America, it stood for a transpartisan, pluralistic development through compromise.

That liberal ideology fills the silence between Hester's cold defiance at the election day ceremony and her final consolation for dissidents. Far from wanting to mute sorrow and perplexity, Hawthorne emphatically gives voice to the wretched to a degree his contemporaries sometimes considered morbid. But he does so to elicit our acquiescence to what he believed was "the remedy," working uncoerced in its own time and ways. In this sense *The Scarlet Letter* may be said to substitute one kind of hiatus or gap for another. I refer to a model of historical irony that stands at the polar extreme from the one I have just discussed: not union through compromise, but regeneration through violence. That variant model was equally rooted in the culture. It may be traced from the Puritans' Wars of the Lord (correlative of their gradual, forever-"preparatory" errand into the wilderness) through the revolutionary summons to independence. "We had been in the steady way of maturation" into nationhood, declared Samuel Sherwood in the most popular sermon of 1776, when suddenly "floods poured from the mouth of the serpent, which at length have brought on a civil war"; and several months earlier, in the most popular pamphlet of that year, Tom Paine contrasted independence (as "growth" and "maturation") with "the least inclination toward a compromise." "Reconciliation," he concluded, "is *now* a fallacious dream." This model of unity through confrontation is inscribed in representative works such as Timothy Dwight's epic of the Revolution, *The Conquest of Canaan*, in cultural keywords such as "manifest destiny," and in large-scale social actions such as the extermination of the Native Americans. The "savages," went the argument, were by definition an "extinct race"–if not now, then "in Heaven's own time"; the issue was not agency but destiny, working itself out either by natural or by human means. Andrew Jackson mobilized the human means; Emerson opted for nature. It was "the great charity of God to the human race," he explained, to prepare for "new individuals and races" by "extinguishing" old ones, and charity should be allowed to take its own course.[30]

In the antebellum North, with the Native American issue fundamentally settled, the debate shifted to the issue of slavery. It is a testament to the flexibility, the volatility, and the resilience of the American symbology that it managed to incorporate both violence and gradualism–indeed, managed to make one a function of the other and each a model of regeneration through consensus. And it seems predictable under these conditions that the metaphysicians of "Indian killing" should have become leading advocates of compromise. Those who supported the resolutions, we recall, wanted nature and providence to usher in what Webster called "the certain destiny that awaits us." Like Emerson, they were awaiting the "great charity of God to the human race." Those who opposed compromise did not deny that certain destiny; they simply wanted to take charity into their own hands. Emerson's famous attack on the Fugitive Slave Act is exemplary. Delivered in 1854, when the negative connotations of "compromise" ("derogatory," "shameful," "disreputable") were beginning to eclipse the "promise" of "mutual concession," as in Frederick Douglass's impassioned appeal for "The End of All Compromises with Slavery—Now and Forever" (May 26, 1854), it warrants extended quotation as the ideological counterpart to Hawthorne's ironies of reconciliation:

> Slavery is disheartening; *but* Nature is not so helpless *but* it can rid itself at last of every wrong. *But* the spasms of Nature are centuries and ages, and will tax the faith of short-lived men. Slowly, slowly the Avenger comes, *but* comes surely. The proverbs of the nations affirm these delays, *but* affirm the arrival. They say, "God may consent, *but* not forever." The delay of the Divine Justice—this was the meaning and soul of the Greek Tragedy. . . .
>
> These delays, you see them now in the . . . torpor [that] exists here . . . on the subject of domestic slavery. . . . Yes, that is the stern edict of Providence, that liberty shall be no hasty fruit, *but* that event on event, population on population, age on age, shall cast itself into the opposite scale, and not until liberty has slowly accumulated weight enough to countervail and preponderate against all this, can the sufficient recoil come. . . .
>
> *Whilst* the inconsistency of slavery with the principles on which the world is built guarantees its downfall, I own that the patience it requires is *almost* too sublime for mortals, and *seems* to demand of us more than mere hoping. And when one sees how fast the rot spreads . . . we demand of superior men that they be superior in this—that the mind and the virtue shall give their verdict in their day, and accelerate so far the progress of civilization. . . . *But* be that sooner or later, I hope we have . . . come to a belief that there is a divine Providence in the world, which will not save us *but* through our own cooperation.[31]

These winding negations and indirections invert Hawthorne's strategy of inaction, but the inversion begins with and returns to a common symbolic outlook. Hawthorne translates the dynamics of process into social integration; Emerson, into cultural renewal. His summons to avenge, like Hawthorne's to patience, mobilizes all the universals on the side of Northern ideology. "Nature," "Divine Justice," "liberty," "the mind," "virtue," "the progress of civilization"—the very "principles on which the world is built" serve to consecrate the Yankee "our."

This sort of troping characterizes the later Emerson. I adduce it here not to deny the radicalism of his great early essays (a subject I take up in the next chapter) but to suggest the remarkable flexibility of American liberal ideology. The "divine Providence" to which Emerson appeals works through essentially the same ironic spirit of history of which Bushnell spoke in 1849, as he did six years earlier in an oration on "The Growth of Law":

> the advanced sentiment of the world, under Christianity, makes it capable of a better and juster practice. . . . It is conceivable that even a positive statute of revelation may lose its applicability, by reason of a radical change in the circumstances it was designed to cover. Nor can it properly be said that such a statute is repealed—it is only waiting for the circumstances in which its virtue lay. A new rule, contradictory to it in words, may yet be wholly consistent with it, and bring no reflection on its merits. Accordingly, in what are called reforms, the real problem more frequently is to revise or mitigate law, perhaps to legislate anew. And there is no evil in the human state, nothing opposed to the general good and happiness, which can not be lawed out of existence.[32]

The sacred-secular hermeneutics this outlook entails, blending cosmic and legal process, informs the views of both Emerson and Pierce, of both Seward and Webster. It conveys the same "spirit as of prophecy" for which Dimmesdale remains and to which Hester returns—Dimmesdale, "to foretell a high and glorious destiny for the newly gathered people of the Lord" (332–33); Hester, to herald "the destined prophetess . . .

angel and apostle of the coming revelation." And in turn that spirit is authorized by the same liberal faith in process that Julia Ward Howe endorsed when, speaking as "angel or apostle" of the Union, she announced: "Mine eyes have seen the glory of the coming of the Lord."[33]

Hawthorne could not have intended the irony this connection implies, one that makes Hester's vision a foreshadowing of "The Battle Hymn of the Republic." And no doubt he would have abhorred that implication if he had foreseen it. Let us call it an unconscious irony, intended by the symbology he inherited. This cultural intention, however defined, finds direct expression in the novel's persistent, if sporadic, rhetoric of violence. Hawthorne's reference to the Revolution makes it integral to the meanings of the A that it is a trophy of war, and this particular meaning is extended through the imagery connecting the introduction to the story proper: for example, the acrimony of self-interest, "where brethren of the same household must diverge from one another," and the prospect of economic and political "warfare," waged in the "fierce and bitter spirit of malice and revenge," "poisoned with ill-will," and, after "seething turmoil," leaving the defeated at "the mercy of a hostile administration" (154–56).

These contrapuntal ambiguities add another level of complexity and control to Hawthorne's design. They give a greater density to his strategy of multiple choice and lend a deeper resonance to the pervasive force of negation, which verges on the dialectical only to veer in the direction of irony. From all these angles they find the right symbolic focus in the national eagle, icon of the Revolution, as Hawthorne describes it in the introduction. An "enormous specimen of the American eagle," he writes, hovered above the customshouse door,

> with outspread wings, a shield before her breast, and a bunch of intermingled thunderbolts and barbed arrows in each claw. With the customary infirmity of temper that characterizes this unhappy fowl, she appears, by the fierceness of her beak and eye and the general trucu-

lency of her attitude, to threaten mischief to the inoffensive community; and especially to warn all citizens, careful of their safety, against intruding on the premises. . . . Nevertheless, vixenly as she looks, many people are seeking, at this very moment, to shelter themselves under the wing of the federal eagle. . . . But she has no great tenderness, even in her best of moods, and, sooner or later,—oftener sooner than late,—is apt to fling off her nestlings with a scratch of her claw, a dab of her beak, or a rankling wound from her barbed arrows. (122–23)

The eagle and the A: for all the oppositions between them, they are symbols made out of the same cultural materials. Both are ambiguous artifacts of authority; both are social emblems transformed by private vision in such a way as simultaneously to assert the self and to accommodate community; and in both cases the act of accommodation recasts the untoward events of history—the "ulcerated wound" of Hester's penance (191), the wounds that Hawthorne received in 1849 from the claw of Whig party functionaries—in terms of art as cultural work. It is the myth of Philoctetes, ironized. And it is appropriate that the two symbols, so ironized, should find common ground in the Salem Customs House—"Uncle Sam's brick edifice" (128), entry to the Republic of 1849, as the Puritans were for Hawthorne the entry to national history. The extraordinary force and cunning of his vision attests to the symbolic resources of what by 1850 was becoming the single most cohesive ideology of the modern world.

Chapter Four

The Paradoxes of Dissent

THE RETURN OF Hester Prynne is problematic not because it makes the novel's close a parable of reconciliation—reconciliation, complementarity, and compromise are the keys to Hawthorne's art—but because, as closure, her return is made the vehicle of process. The conclusion brings together all the novel's tendencies toward "mutual concession," but every "fact" in it resists integration. The A on Dimmesdale's breast, the authority of the Ur-manuscript, the testimony of "contemporary witnesses," the manner of Chillingworth's death, the relation between the doctor and the minister, the fate of Pearl, and finally the meanings of the double grave site and the tombstone's heraldic motto (340–45)—one after another the details that surround and attend Hester's compromise subvert closure. Near the start of this chapter Hawthorne tells us of the scarlet letter that he "would gladly, now that it has done its office, erase its deep print out of [his] own brain" (340), but even that wish for finality works to open (rather than resolve) questions about the letter's office.

This emphasis on process, we have seen, is central to Hawthorne's strategy of cohesion. Critics of modernism and postmodernism speak of the "constitutive uncertainty" of literary ambiguity, with its indeterminate "obliquity of signs" and "inconclusive luxuriance of meaning."[1] *The Scarlet Letter* reconstitutes inconclusiveness, in all its luxuriant uncertainty of meaning, into a unified design, grounded in the dynamics of liberal culture: the necessary friction between private interest and the public good; the ironies of personal agency; and the ambiguities of group pluralism through which consensus is established and sustained.

Still, the sheer volatility of process in *The Scarlet Letter* warrants investigation in its own right. Hawthorne's methods entail a principle of resistance, an overriding concern with negation, that suggests another, contrary element at the core of his art. For purposes of analysis, I will call this element "paradox," as distinct from ambiguity: "*paradox* . . . a statement or proposition seemingly self-contradictory or absurd, and yet explicable as expressing a truth; any person or thing exhibiting apparent contradictions"; "*ambiguity* . . . open to various interpretations . . . equivocal." Now as at 1850,[2] this makes for a distinction in degree, not in kind, and, as such, it is crucial to Hawthorne's method. His symbols tend ambiguously toward reciprocity, yet, paradoxically, they tend to resist integration in every form. We see this in Pearl, who is the agent in extremis both of synthesis, "the scarlet letter endowed with life" (204), and of repudiation, to the point of repudiating the New World altogether. We see it, too, in the author of "The Custom-House," who presents himself as the very essence of relatedness (past and present, artist and community, private and public) and simultaneously as a figure of utter disavowal—of his native Salem, of his official post, of his Puritan forebears, of friends and enemies alike ("how little time it has taken to disconnect me from them all"), and, figuratively, as the "DECAPITATED SURVEYOR," of "all the world!" (156–57). The customshouse is the community he abandons at the end, as Pearl abandons Boston in 1649. "The Custom-House" is his own elaborately embroidered letter to the reader, and, like Hester, he returns to it after all—much as he returns to the letter he had dropped shuddering upon the customshouse floor ("as if [it] were not of red cloth, but red-hot iron" [146])—not only in the conclusion, but again, with special emphasis on its "effect of the truth," in his preface to the second edition:

> Much to the author's surprise, and (if he may say so without additional offence) considerably to his amusement, he finds that his sketch of official life, introductory to THE SCARLET LETTER, has created an unprecedented excitement in the respectable community immediately around him. It could hardly have been more violent indeed, had he burned down the Custom-House. . . . As the public disapprobation would weigh very heavily on him, were he conscious of deserving it, the author begs leave to say, that he has carefully read over the introductory pages, with a purpose to alter or expunge whatever might be found amiss, and to make the best reparation in his power for the atrocities of which he has been adjudged guilty. But it appears to him . . . that it could not have been done in a better or kindlier spirit, nor . . . with a livelier effect of the truth.
>
> The author is constrained, therefore, to republish his introductory sketch without the change of a word.
>
> SALEM, *March 30, 1850* (119)

The passage is characteristic of Hawthorne's use of paradox. On the one hand, it attests to his engagement with community. Its assertiveness is a sign of deference; its acerbity, a poignant expression of the same impulse to vindicate his public role as author, which animates "The Custom-House" at large. On the other hand, that very impulse serves (as in "The Custom-House") to highlight his self-conscious connection to his *radical* heroine. I refer, first, to the adversarial Hester midway through the novel, subjected like the author to "violent . . . public disapprobation" and scorning those by whom she had "been adjudged guilty." More broadly, I refer to the prophet at the end, who comes back to reconsecrate her dream of love. For, like Hawthorne, Hester never really submits to the public. One reason (we have seen) that we accept her return is that the narrator has prepared us for it by his persistent criticism of her self-reliance. But her terms of acceptance (her insistence on resuming the A in spite of the magistrates' change of heart) also confirm our sense of her persisting willfulness and courage. If anything, her newfound humility seems to strengthen her former resolve. According to Surveyor Pue, Hester not only does "whatever miscellaneous good she might," as before, but now takes "it upon herself to give advice in all matters" so that, for all the "reverence" paid her by "many people," some at least consider her "an intruder and a nuisance" (146). And Hawthorne makes it clear that her advice, far from reversing her old convictions, draws out their boldest implications. Hester magnifies what before had been merely personal, a summons to flight, into a vision of universal progress: "the whole relation" she foresees "between man and woman," verified by "the truest test of a life successful to such an end," is now the sure sign of a "brighter period" to come.

These *subversive* continuities between the earlier and the later Hester—between the self-styled martyr and the still-defiant apostle of compromise—cannot be said to undermine the integrity of Hawthorne's vision, but they do lend it a certain explosive potential. To recall the dictionary definition of "paradox," they add to the complexity of the final ambiguous "truth" a "seemingly self-contradictory" emphasis on what has *not* been reconciled. They remind us, for example, that Hester's prophecy, like her penitence to be, is grounded in her former discontents. The comfort she gives—to "women, more especially, . . . in the continually recurring trials of wounded, wasted, wronged, misplaced or erring and sinful passion" (344)—pointedly evokes her recalcitrance midway through the novel. Her antagonism then to "the world's law" contrasts with her final acquiescence, but the contrast also enhances her abiding "freedom of speculation." Indeed, it may be seen to lend a new heroic dimension to her self-reliance. Hester's "scorn and bitterness" drop away (344); her sorrow is attended by a ripeness of wisdom and experience; and her enthusiasm for change is all the more persuasive for her stoic recognition of necessity.

In all this Hester's tragic stature highlights the enormous hope invested in her dissent, a hope that remains compelling in spite of the narrator's running quarrel with radicalism itself, as our admiration for her independence grows through the novel in spite of his warnings against its growing tendencies to excess. When at the end Hester takes up her "stigma" again (344), it resonates for us, paradoxically, with the antithetical force of her declaration of independence during her forest meeting with Dimmesdale:

"What we did had a consecration of its own. We felt it so! We said so to each other!" (286)

Hawthorne writes that Hester's "whole seven years of outlaw and ignominy had been little other than a preparation for this very hour" (291), and it would not be inaccurate to see in this apotheosis of her rebellion—situated midway between "Another View of Hester" and the novel's conclusion—the thematic counterpoint to the A's office of constraint. To that end, upon Hester's return Hawthorne calls attention to the repressions of "that iron period" (344). The solace that Hester now offers draws sustenance from her regeneration then, however fleeting, when she broke the "bondage" of "these iron men and their opinions" (291, 288):

"Do I feel joy again?" cried [Dimmesdale], wondering at himself. "Methought the germ of it was dead in me! O Hester, thou art my better angel! I seem to have flung myself—sick, sin-stained, and sorrow-blackened—down upon these forest leaves, and to have risen up all made anew, and with new powers to glorify Him that hath been merciful! This is already the better life! Why did we not find it sooner?"

"Let us not look back," answered Hester Prynne. "The past is gone! Wherefore should we linger upon it now? See! With this symbol, I undo it all, and make it as it had never been!"

So speaking, she undid the clasp that fastened the scarlet letter. . . . (292)

That act of abandonment is the paradigmatic expression of the absolute, unyielding dissent that characterizes Hester both at the end and during the course of the novel. We are occasionally told, vaguely and abstractly, about her wild freedom of speculation, but only at this moment do her thoughts take active and overt form. We hear of Hester's defiance throughout the novel, as we sense rather than see her "radiant and tender" femininity (293), but only in this visible undoing of social clasps—clearly, the forecast of her one other open gesture of defiance, when she departs for Europe (which Hawthorne pointedly does *not* describe)—does her sweeping contempt for "whatever priests or legislators had established" (290) finally find an appropriate symbolic action. And it is pertinent to Hawthorne's use of paradox that he should direct our views of its appropriateness through the discrepancy we feel (throughout the novel, but here most dramatically) between our admiration for Hester and the novel's disapproving commentary. The narrator tells us that when Hester discards the A the little brook nearby breaks into a

> merry gleam . . . which had [now] become a mystery of joy.
>
> Such was the sympathy of Nature—that wild, heathen Nature of the forest, never subjugated by human law, nor illuminated by higher truth, . . . (192)

but we endorse "the sympathy of Nature" nonetheless and participate with Hester in its "mystery of joy."

The discrepancy is exemplary among other reasons because it cannot be ascribed to an unreliable narrator. Quite the contrary: all ancillary evidence (from letters, journals, sketches, and conversations) suggests a rather exact correspondence between Hawthorne's views and the critique (not mere condemnation) of radicalism in *The Scarlet Letter.* That Hawthorne differs from his narrator is implicit in his very use of a persona. The issue is not whether Hawthorne *is* the narrator but what the difference between the author and narrator signifies. Hence, the pertinence of Hawthorne's use of paradox and, more accurately, the distinction in degree he assumes between paradox and ambiguity—paradox as a variant type of ambiguity, providing a source of sustained tension within an overall aesthetic-cultural design. Hawthorne's authorial persona is neither an attempt on his part to set us in opposition to the narrator nor the site of dialogic conflict between author and character.* Rather it is part of an intricate pattern of meaning that makes paradox (and all that it implies) integral to the office of *The Scarlet Letter.* Hawthorne evokes the threat of discontinuity; he elicits conflict in interpretation—as in the forest scene, deliberately highlighting the disparity between the narrator's conservatism and our sympathy for Hester—in order to convey the benefits both of community for the dissenter and of dissent for the community. Indeed, he elaborates upon those double blessings at every turn of the novel, from the first, when Hester pushes aside the beadle and complies with the law "of her own free-will," to the last, when she transforms her compliance into a sweeping reaffirmation of the tensions between the need for self-fulfillment and the claims of society. It hardly exaggerates the case to say that her return provides resolution precisely by magnifying those tensions, pro-

*"Pseudo-dialogic" might be a better term, since the presupposition continues to be authorial control, now with the narrator as foil. Thus, Austin Warren distinguishes the "real" Hawthorne (who happens to be as antisentimentalist as Warren himself) from the untrustworthy "commentator, the husband of Sophia" ("*The Scarlet Letter:* A Literary Exercise in Moral Theology," *Southern Review* 1 [1965]: 30), and Michael J. Colacurcio reads the narrator's reproval of Hester in the forest scene as being "Hawthorne's relentless deconstruction" of "Hester's metaphorical bondage" to a patriarchal society ("'The Woman's Own Choice': Sex, Metaphor, and the Puritan 'Sources' of *The Scarlet Letter,*" in *New Essays on "The Scarlet Letter,"* ed. Michael J. Colacurcio [Cambridge: Cambridge University Press, 1985], 122). This is to turn the intentional fallacy on its head, but the results are not necessarily less fallacious. The old view was that if the narrator said it the author meant it; the new view is that if we do not agree the author must have meant something else. The license this gives to pluralist interpretation—a license (among other things) to create an interpretive gap through which we can attribute our concerns and beliefs to the secret "true" author—has certain affinities to Hawthorne's techniques, but it does not therefore bring us closer to *The Scarlet Letter.*

jecting them, as the very spirit of prophecy, into the realm of utopia and millennium.

I said earlier that the office of the A is socialization. I would now add that for Hawthorne (and his culture) socialization is a matter not of repressing radical energies but of redirecting them, in all their radical force, into a continuing opposition between self and society. It is no accident that those terms of opposition have dominated the response to the novel. Nothing more clearly testifies to the power of Hawthorne's directives for interpretation than the persistence with which for almost a century and a half—from the vantage points, successively, of morality (or religion), psychology, mythology, and aesthetics—critics have sought to resolve, clarify, or enlarge upon the polarity of self and society in *The Scarlet Letter*.* And nothing more clearly testifies to the reciprocities of text and context than the persistence with which they have identified the self in that polarity, positively or negatively (or both), with the doctrine of radical individualism.

We admire Hester neither for her antinomian tendencies (in any sectarian sense), nor for her feminism, nor for any other theological or political heresies embedded in her defiance, and not even (or not primarily) for her attributes as mother and

*The reviewers of 1850 tended to arraign themselves on one side or the other, either praising society for upholding "convention" and "moral laws" (Anne W. Abbott in *North American Review* and Orestes Brownson in *Brownson's Quarterly Review*) or else commending Hester for her "heroic traits" and "great self-sustaining properties" of character (George Bailey Loring in *Massachusetts Quarterly Review* and E. P. Whipple in *Graham's Magazine*). By the late nineteenth century it had become commonplace to interpret the conflict as a universal tension between self and society, and most subsequent criticism has followed that pattern, which predictably shifts with changing aesthetic or intellectual currents: from "realistic" or psychological in the 1920s through archetypal or existential in the 1950s to (say) recent feminist studies by Nina Baym, *The Scarlet Letter: A Reading* (Boston: Twayne, 1986); and Louise De Salvo, *Nathaniel Hawthorne* (Atlantic Highlands, N.J.: Humanities Press International, 1987). It amounts to a sustained tribute to the power of Hawthorne's directives for interpretation.

lover, but for what we feel to be her heroic self-reliance, an extraordinary independence of spirit manifested with increasing force through the novel, and doubly reinforced at the end by her capacity to transform remembrances of social wrongs past (and evidence of present social injustice) into a vision of future *self*-realization: "a woman . . . lofty, pure, and beautiful," "a life successful to such an end!" Hawthorne invites us in the first chapter to compare Hester with "the sainted Anne Hutchinson." We might say that the problem of dissent in *The Scarlet Letter* lies in the paradox of Hester's sainted individualism.

That paradox is best symbolized by the discarded/restored A; the problem of dissent it entails is articulated most fully in Hester's impassioned forest appeal, which Hawthorne extends over two chapters: "The Pastor and His Parishioner," where the lovers meet, and "A Flood of Sunshine," where they decide to leave New England. At the center, as though to dramatize the dynamics of cause and effect, he reviews Hester's radical development. It is a brief but highly suggestive interlude, evoking all the "shadowy [Old World] guests . . . perilous as demons" who had tempted her through her "seven years of outlaw" (259). Hawthorne describes her "mind of native courage and activity," recalls how she "had habituated herself" to an extraordinary "latitude of speculation," and tells us that "she looked from this estranged point of view at human institutions, and whatever priests or legislators had established; criticizing all"—a criticism (we have seen) that takes in "the clerical band, the judicial robe . . . the fireside . . . [and] the church."

Now, the impulse behind Hester's appeal to Dimmesdale is entirely different; it has to do not with social change but with inner regeneration and unhampered personal process ("Let us not look back. . . . The past is gone!"). But Hawthorne insists on the continuity as well as the contrast between the two radical modes. Insofar as they contrast, we are made to see that, as radical heroine, Hester casts out the demons of European revolt and liberates *herself.* Insofar as the two radical modes are continuous, her heroism consists in her capacity to recast those demons into the energies of the radical self. The paradox hinges here on the double meaning of selfhood, as self-sustaining and as adversarial, and from this double perspective, in "The Pastor and His Parishioner," Hester summons Dimmesdale to his "true" identity: "Preach! Write! Act! Do anything," so long as it is *your* thing; do it under any name, so long as what you do is "truly yours," and do it anywhere—in an Indian settlement, "in some remote rural village or in vast London . . . in Germany, in France, in pleasant Italy"—so long as you will not feel "hemmed in" (288–91). Hester's appeal is her own most moving justification, the fit expression of her self-consecrated love:

> "Thou art crushed under this seven-years' weight of misery," replied Hester, fervently resolved to buoy him up with her own energy. . . . "Begin all anew! Hast thou exhausted possibility in the failure of this one trial? Not so! The future is yet full of trial and success! There is happiness to be enjoyed! There is good to be done! Exchange this false life of thine for a true one. . . . Up and away!"
>
> "O Hester!" cried Arthur Dimmesdale. . . . "There is not the strength or courage left me to venture into the wide, strange, difficult world, alone!" . . .
>
> He repeated the word.
>
> "Alone, Hester!"
>
> "Thou shalt not go alone!" answered she, in a deep whisper.
>
> Then, all was spoken! (288–89)

This is a lovers' reunion, a pledge of mutual dependence, and no doubt readers have sometimes responded in these terms, if only by association with other texts. But in *this* text the focus of our response is the individual, not the couple (or the family). Over a century and a half of criticism testifies that the force of love in the forest scene attracts mainly as a force for self-reliance. As a reviewer of 1850 put it:

> While Arthur Dimmesdale, cherished in the arms of that society which he had outraged . . . was dying of an inward anguish, Hester stood upon her own true ground . . . learning that true wisdom which

comes through honesty and self-justification. . . . This bore her through her trial; and this . . . tore the scarlet letter from her breast, and made her young and pure again.[3]

The "true ground" and "true wisdom" of self-justification: the statement is extreme for its time (or ours), but it reflects the dominant sense of Hester's heroism. What emerges when all is spoken is her resolve to go it alone, defiantly, to the point of bearing the minister's aloneness as well. This is the import as well (to judge from reader response) in what Hester calls "*our* love" and "what *we* said": its true ground and wisdom are finally her own.* It is *her* passion and will we admire in both instances, her determination "to buoy him up with her own energy," perhaps even to infuse Dimmesdale with an energy of his own, as indeed she does (although, paradoxically, it works against her plan of flight), precisely by giving him "the strength or courage," such as it is, "to venture into the . . . difficult world, alone." As for Hester herself, this spirit of the new carries her, in "A Flood of Sunshine," to the climactic self-affirmation I quoted earlier:

So speaking, she undid the clasp that fastened the scarlet letter and, taking it from her bosom, threw it to a distance among the withered leaves. The mystic token alighted on the hither verge of the stream. With a hand's breadth farther flight it would have fallen into the water, and have given the little brook another woe to carry onward, besides the unintelligible tale which it still kept murmuring about.

*The impact of the forest scene can be traced in these terms from the first reviews, but in institutional terms that scene becomes a key text through the criticism of George Parsons Lathrop, William Dean Howells, Henry James, and Paul Elmer More. Frederic I. Carpenter's view is fairly representative: "she embodies the authentic American dream of a new life . . . and of self-reliant action to that ideal" ("Scarlet A Minus," *College English* 5 [January 1944]: 179). In one form or another, this view is adopted even by those critics who see the novel in conventional romance terms: "Hester is . . . one of the two principal antagonists in the drama, the Puritan community being the other," while Dimmesdale's importance lies in the fact that "the issue between Hester and the town come to a focus in him" (Ernest Sandeen, "*The Scarlet Letter* as a Love Story," *PMLA* 77 [September, 1962]: 434).

> But there lay the embroidered letter, glittering like a lost jewel. . . .
> The stigma gone, Hester heaved a long, deep sigh, in which the burden of shame and anguish departed from her spirit. . . . By another impulse, she took off the formal cap that confined her hair; and down it fell upon her shoulders, dark and rich . . . imparting the charm of softness to her features. There played around her mouth, and beamed out of her eyes, a radiant and tender smile, that seemed gushing from the very heart of womanhood. . . . Her sex, her youth, and the whole richness of her beauty, came back from what men call the irrevocable past, and clustered themselves, with her maiden hope, and a happiness before unknown, within the magic circle of this hour. . . . All at once, as with a sudden smile of heaven, forth burst the sunshine, pouring a very flood into the obscure forest, gladdening each green leaf, transmuting the yellow fallen ones to gold, and gleaming adown the gray trunks of the solemn trees. (292–93)

The scarlet letter had not (yet) done its office: Pearl must retrieve it and, later still, Hester herself. In this sense the A buried "among the withered leaves" is a forecast of her return. But its office is palpably, dramatically already underway, and in a more direct sense—as well as in a more compelling fashion, to judge from reader response—the ritual of rebirth is complete "within the magic circle of this hour." As the "yellow fallen" leaves are "transmuted into gold," Hester emerges, phoenix-like, out of the ashes of social stigma. It is the fulfillment of Dimmesdale's wished-for rebirth ("O Hester, thou art my better angel! I seem to have . . . risen up all made anew") and a forecast in turn not only of Hester the prophet but, beyond that, of the angel of prophecy herself. Now as then, Puritan society disappears, along with "shame and anguish." Only nature remains, in all its inner and actual richness, together with the natural self, "radiant" with "maiden hope and a happiness before unknown," under the "smile of heaven."

This striking parallel between what we might consider the novel's twin epiphanies—our revelation of Hester in the forest and Hester's revelation of pure womanhood at the end—attests to narrative cohesion. And yet in the context of the forest scene that same parallel works to disavow all connection whatever. Like the discarded A, Hester's act of negation brings her to "the hither verge" of radicalism. It so vividly affirms the individual and, as an act prepared for by Hester's "whole seven years," so deliberately invests her radicalism with a consecration of its own that we must acknowledge a discrepancy in the letter's very office. The A on her bosom mediates between society and the resisting individual. The "mystic token" at the river's edge is a symbol of resistance in itself; it tends to undo (rather than reconcile) polarities—to separate process from telos, pluralism from consensus, the adversarial from the integrated self.

I have labeled this form of radicalism "dissent" because the term seems to me best to convey its distinctive qualities: processual, negational, and personal. Like the scarlet letter, it is a cultural artifact that is both counterdependent and independent, bound to society in symbiotic antagonism and, at the same time, infused with an absolutist vision of its own. This dual quality accounts for the emphasis on process: it is the office of dissent to challenge (subvert, combat, and deny) the power of consensus it represents. And, as we have seen, it sustains its force of negation through an equally pronounced tendency to personalize the challenge. To endorse Hester as radical is to believe that social change follows from self-realization, not vice versa; that true revolution is therefore an issue of individual growth rather than group action; and that the conflict it entails between self and society centers not on schemes for institutional change, whether by reform or transformation, but on the freedom of the individual "to begin anew"—which is to say, on one's resistance to all institutional controls.

These are the tenets of Hester's sainted individualism. They are also the principles by which our classic writers distinguished American radicalism from the tradition that they, along with other spokesmen for the culture, identified as Old World revolution. They did not simply repudiate the European Forty-eight. Each of them, partly through that act of repudiation, forged a subversive mode of his own. *Walden*'s Thoreau, Whitman's Walt, and Melville's Ishmael and Ahab are representative, each in his unique way, of the paradoxes implicit in Hester's self-assertion. So, too, in his way, is the radically self-made hero of *The Narrative of Frederick Douglass;* so, also, mutatis mutandis, the socially resistant, culturally conformist protagonists of *Uncle Tom's Cabin* and *The Wide, Wide World.* The central instance is Emerson, of course. I have in mind our current proto-Nietzschean, neopragmatist Emerson—not the heir of Anne Hutchinson, but the self-generated precursor of William James—seer of "perpetual inchoation" and rhapsodist of nonconformity, prophet of "the new" as "transition" set against "repose" in any form, set against telos itself:

> The new continents are built out of the ruins of an old planet; the new races fed out of the decomposition of the foregoing. New arts destroy the old. . . . Every thing looks permanent until its secret is known. . . . Every ultimate fact is only the first of a series. . . . Every one seems to be contradicted by the new; it is only limited by the new. The new statement is always hated by the old. . . . A new degree of culture would instantly revolutionize the entire system of human pursuits. . . . No love can be bound by oath or covenant to secure it against a higher love. No truth so sublime but it may be trivial tomorrow in the light of new thoughts. . . . I cast away in this new moment all my once hoarded knowledge, as vacant and vain . . . [and] make a new road to new and better goals.[4]

This passage from Emerson's "Circles" typifies the radical individualism of *Essays: First Series* (1841). It also typifies the spirit behind Hester's defense of her "higher love" and, more broadly, her summons to undo the past—to revolutionize by opening, contradicting, unbinding, and casting away, and so to transform what seemed to be ultimate into the first in a new series of possibilities. One could find no better gloss on the discarded A as symbol than the strategies by which, in his great early essays, Emerson establishes the absolute dichotomy of self and society. He images fulfillment as multiple circles of independence—self-generated, self-contained infinities. He transforms earlier concepts of autonomy (René Descartes's cogito, John Locke's self-possessive individualism) into a self-emptying mode of "visionary possession," one that requires us to discard in order to incorporate. He insists on risk at all cost, especially the cost of social stability. He advocates self-reliance in order to unsettle cultural norms. His concept of progress is predicated on the repudiation of society: "the individual mind always advances. . . . Society is, as men of the world have always found it, tumultuous, insecure, unprincipled."[5]

Emerson's brilliant colonial progenitor, Peter Bulkeley, set out the Puritan scheme of preparation I mentioned in chapter 1 in connection with Hester's return: the rigorous step-by-step progress toward oneness-in-Christ. We might describe Emersonian individualism, along with Hester's forest appeal, as an antischematic preparation for dissent. "If I am the Devil's child," Emerson declares in a passage that reads like Pearl at her most perverse, "I will live then from the Devil"; again, in what seems almost a parody of Hester's justification of her adultery: "The only sin is limitation"; and once again, in a set of aphorisms that might be said to combine Hester's twin epiphanies (first in the forest, then at the end): "A man contains all that is needful to his government within himself. He is made a law unto himself. . . . All that a man has thought or achieved, [however,] be it never so wise and brave, is but initial, is only the first gropings of the giant that shall be. . . . And out of the strength and wisdom of the private heart shall go forth at another era the regeneration of society."[6]

From the start readers of *The Scarlet Letter* recognized and debated this Emersonian strain in the novel. Some went so far as to call Hawthorne a secret transcendentalist or, like Poe, a transcendentalist in spite of his own best self. That is too far, I believe. I would suggest instead a contextual web of influence: Hester's dissent is a major dramatization of certain developments within antebellum culture that found their fullest expression in Emerson's radical concept of the self. At the center of these developments is the transatlantic controversy over the term "individualism." The differences between Hawthorne and Emerson are well known, and they are perhaps nowhere sharper than in the matter of self-reliance. In pointing to the parallels between them, I do not mean to blur those differences but to highlight the breadth and richness of the cultural symbology they shared. Hester's dissent may be said to represent a mainstream liberal version of the debate over individualism. Emerson's gradual formulation of the concept through the 1840s is the best single index we have to the issues at stake.

"Individualism" was coined in the early 1820s by French opponents of laissez-faire to designate the modern evils—"ruthless competition," "infinite fragmentation," "mean egoism"—that they believed were "undermining the political and social order." In this wholly pejorative sense, the term was adopted by most nineteenth-century critics of liberal society and, in particular, by the radical sectaries whom we have come to call (after Karl Marx) utopian socialists. Among these were the Fourierists, who inspired the Brook Farm experiment, and the Saint-Simonians who shaped the official dictionary definitions of individualism, beginning in 1834: "system of those who considered society to be no more than an aggregation of individuals, and the state to have no rights in itself"; "the exclusive domination of capital, the reign of the bourgeois aristocracy"; and "theory by which the rights of the individual prevail over those of society." These definitions were aimed polemically against the middle classes of Europe and ethnographically, as the description of a way of life, against the Northern United States.[7]

The American response is a testament to the maturation of Jacksonian ideology. By 1840 the assault on individualism had provoked a sweeping counterattack against Old World traditions that issued in a wholesale redefinition of the term. In America, as nowhere else, individualism came to signify a set of social ideals and, more than that, a political and economic system destined to bring society to "ultimate perfection."* This outlook contrasts not only with the European critique but with Emerson's adversarial ideal. The Jacksonian ideologues upheld individualism institutionally (as, in fact, the term then required) as a way of life that was bringing to fruition the "great progressive movement," from the "state of savage individualism to that of an individualism more elevated, moral, and refined."[8] For Emerson individualism centered first and last on the independent self. Progress for him was a function of self-reliance working against the ubiquitous conspiracies of society.

The proper term for this outlook, we know, is "individuality," the belief in the absolute integrity, spiritual primacy, and inviolable sanctity of the self. In the neutral distinction of the mid-century *Nouveau Dictionnaire Universel,* individualism meant "system of isolation [of isolated selves], in work or in undertakings, the opposite of the spirit of association," whereas individuality, a category of "Philosophy," pointed to "what constitutes the individual. What makes the individual himself, what gives him a distinct existence. . . . Every thinking being knows its individuality." A number of scholars have discussed Emerson's thought from that perspective but mainly from within a national context, as expressing its relation to

*Characteristically, the apologia for individualism is set within the framework of American ironic historiography: "Individualism was . . . the free spirit of the new-born democracy . . . [in] a land . . . prepared [for this purpose by God] in the solitudes of the Western hemisphere. And, then, the men sufficient to accomplish the work needed to be particular men. . . . men of the pilgrim stock . . . [who] asserted with remarkable directness and force the great doctrines of popular sovereignty, of political equality, of sacred individual rights" ("Course of Civilization," *United States Magazine and Democratic Review* 6 [September, 1839]: 211–12). In a separate study of Emersonian dissent, I try to relate this version of individualism to its broader transatlantic and transhistorical context—what Thomas C. Heller and David E. Wellbury call the "contingent and paradoxical" concepts that shaped the Western "cultural system of individualism" (Introduction to *Reconstructing Individualism: Autonomy, Individuality, and the Self in Western Thought,* ed. Heller, Marton Sosna, and Wellbury [Stanford, Calif.: Stanford University Press, 1986], 3–4).

American liberalism. It is therefore worth stressing that individuality in its modern sense is neither American nor liberal, but European and radical: a transhistorical ideal of self-realization that was developed explicitly, sometimes programmatically, against the perceived defects of systemic individualism. As such, it served as a utopian rallying point for all groups in the political spectrum, from royalists to anarchists. Its influence helps explain the antibourgeois animus behind the European Romantic vision of the individual. Its effects extend from Marx's contrast in the *Grundrisse* between capitalist alienation and "free individuality, based on the universal development of individuals," to John Stuart Mill's invocation of individuality against the encroachments of "the majority," "public opinion," and "the middle class." And, as we might expect, it proved most amenable to the most antiliberal extremes: on the one hand, the elitism of hero worship, from Thomas Carlyle through Nietzsche; on the other hand, the left-wing egalitarianism that eventuated in the revolutions of 1848. "Beware of confounding individuality with individualism," warned the Saint-Simonian Alexandre de Saint-Cherón, echoing a host of radical thinkers from Friedrich List to Max Stirner and Henri Joncière; "individualism is . . . an instrument only for liberating the bourgeoisie," whereas individuality means the full "equality and brotherhood of man," as the influential theorist Pierre Leroux put it in his treatise "On Individualism and Socialism":

> Every man is indeed a fruit on the tree of humanity; but being the product of the tree makes the fruit no less complete and perfect in and of itself. The fruit is also the tree, it contains the seeds of the tree which generated it. . . . Thus in his essence every man is a reflection of society at large, every man is in a certain sense the expression of his century, of his people and of his generation, every man is humanity, every man is a sovereign state, every man is the law for which laws are made and against which no law can prevail.[9]

The parallels to Emerson are obvious enough. But, unlike the Europeans, Emerson never turned individuality against individualism. Instead, he transformed antithesis into paradox by infusing the concept of individualism with the transcendence of individuality. That union of ideology and utopia empowered his radical vision of the self from 1836 to 1841. It also propelled his shift during the mid-1840s toward the conservatism of his later writings. The volatility that this implies speaks directly to the dual office of the A as the symbol of personal dissent (designating "our" radical Hester) and the symbol of the bonds of society (designating the narrator's heroine of compromise). Its cultural significance is made explicit in Emerson's first confrontation with the concept of individualism—in effect, his first response to the challenge of socialist thought and practice.

As it happens, the confrontation coincides with a series of discussions he had with Hawthorne, from September, 1842, through the winter of 1844. Hawthorne had just left Brook Farm, married, and settled at the Old Manse, part of the Emerson family property in Concord, Massachusetts, and both men left records of their talks together as well as of their overnight visit to a Shaker community. Unfortunately, the records are sporadic, but a main topic of conversation seems to have been socialism, a catchall neologism of the time for any collectivist or associationist scheme for radical change, from the Shakers and Brook Farm to German communism. Evidently, too, the two men discussed by contrast the prospect of liberalism—another neologism of the time—identified with Northern society and, more broadly (as they drew out its consequences), with the United States as "the country of the Future" and Jacksonian society as the marketplace of universal desire. As Emerson put it in 1844, the American marketplace is "an Intelligence Office where every man may find what he wishes to buy, and expose what he has to sell," or, in the words of Hawthorne's "The Intelligence Office" (1844), it is a "Central Office, where all human wishes seemed to be made known, and . . . negotiated to their fulfillment."[10]

Predictably, Emerson plays the optimist to Hawthorne's skeptic. It is a distinction in degree, not in kind—Hawthorne mocks his own (obsessive) concern with progress and Emerson worries that the Brook Farmers' "impulse is guarded by no old, old Intellect"—but here as elsewhere that distinction in kind (as between paradox and ambiguity) issues in real differences in outlook. In "The Custom-House" Hawthorne sarcastically compares Emerson's "subtile influence" over him in 1841–44 with his own "fellowship of toil" among "the dreamy brethren of Brook Farm"—though it is a wistful sarcasm, tinged with sympathy for "the struggle of the race for a better and purer life" (140).* Emerson for his part all but submerges his often-professed conservatism ("those in the Conservative side have as much truth & progressive force as those on the Liberal"), along with his distaste for the Brook Farmers' "intellectual Sansculottism," in what may be counted the earliest formulation of radical individualism in the modern world:

*This is from the 1846 sketch "The Hall of Fantasy," which I assume refers to Hawthorne's Brook Farm experience. I assume, too, that the skeptical narrator here expresses something of Hawthorne's sentiments: "Yet, withal, the heart of the staunchest conservative . . . could hardly have helped throbbing in sympathy" with "the herd of real or self-styled reformers that peopled this place of refuge. . . . Be the individual theory as wild as fancy could make it, still the wiser spirit would recognize" the basis for their hope, and "my faith revived even while I rejected all their schemes" (*Tales and Sketches,* ed. Roy Harvey Pearce [New York: Library of America, 1982], 740–41]). To some extent, that faith persisted even after Hawthorne decided (as he wrote on May 25, 1842), that he could "best attain the higher ends of life by retaining the ordinary relation to society" (*The Letters, 1813–1843* Centenary Edition, ed. Thomas Woodson, L. Neal Smith, and Norman Holmes Pearson [Columbus: Ohio State University Press, 1984], 15:624). Emerson was then seeking to undo that "ordinary relation," but he was skeptical enough to take shrewd notice of the Brook Farmers' design: "The 'Community' of socialism is only the continuation of the same movement which made the joint stock companies for manufacturers, mining, insurance, banking, & the rest. It has turned out cheaper to make calico by companies, & it is proposed to bake bread & to roast mutton by companies, & it will be tried & done" (Journal U [November, 1843], in *The Journals of Ralph Waldo Emerson,* ed. Ralph H. Orth and Alfred R. Ferguson [Cambridge, Mass.: Harvard University Press, 1971], 9:54–55).

The young people, like [Orestes] Brownson, [William Henry] Channing, [Christopher A.] Green, E[lizabeth]. P[almer]. P[eabody]., & possibly [George] Bancroft think that the vice of the age is to exaggerate individualism, & they adopt the word *l'humanité* from Le Roux [Pierre Leroux] and go for "*the race*." Hence the Phalanx [promulgated by Charles Fourier], owenism [the doctrines of Robert Dale Owen], Simonism [the doctrines of Count Claude Henri de Saint-Simon], the Communities [such as Brook Farm]. The same spirit in theology has produced the Puseyism [after Edward Pusey, a leader of the Oxford Neocatholics] which endeavors to rear "the Church" as a balance and overpoise to Conscience.

The world is waking up to the idea of Union and already we have Communities, Phalanxes and Aesthetic Families, & Pestalozzian institutions. It is & will be magic. Men will live & communicate & ride & plough & reap & govern as by lightning and galvanic & ethereal power. . . . But this Union is to be reached by a reverse of the methods they use. It is spiritual and must not be actualized. The Union is only perfect when all the Uniters are absolutely isolated. Each man being the Universe, if he attempts to join himself to others, he instantly is jostled, crowded, cramped, halved, quartered, or on all sides diminished of his proportion. . . . But let him go alone, & recognizing the Perfect in every moment with entire obedience he will go up & down doing the works of a true *member,* and, to the astonishment of all, the whole work will be done with concert, though no man spoke; government will be adamantine without any governor.

union ideal,—in actual individualism, actual union

then would be the culmination of science, useful art, fine art, & culmination on culmination.[11]

These two journal entries, dating from late November and/or early December 1842, mark Emerson's first use of the word with which he has rightly been most identified. "Individualism" hovers in both entries between paradox and ambiguity, neither joining the ideal and the actual nor denying their conjunction. Emerson does not endorse the socialist critique, as expressed by the young Brook Farm enthusiasts (such as Brownson, Channing, Greene, and Peabody) and well represented by Pierre Leroux, who coined the term "socialism." But neither does Emerson defend systemic individualism. Indeed, in the second, longer entry he decidedly associates utopia with the socialists' "idea of Union," although (in another reversal) decidedly not with their practices ("the reverse of their methods"). These intricate qualifications find their epitome in the lacuna or hiatus he leaves between "union ideal" and what appears to be its antithesis: "actual individualism, actual union." Logically and grammatically, this one-line paragraph (for which the whole passage seems to have been the preparation) calls for an "ideal individualism." Emerson's hesitation suggests his resistance to Jacksonian ideology—his aversion indeed to investing the ideal in any system, whether that of the liberal North or the Fourierist phalanx. The real point, it would seem, is not socialism versus individualism. It is "perfect union," based on a dream of individuality, something "spiritual and not to be actualized," which by definition sets the individual at odds with society as it is, anywhere, at any time.

And at the same time Emerson's hesitation bespeaks his attraction to the liberal ideal, an attraction implicit in his sweeping attack on socialism—in every country (Switzerland, Italy, Germany, France, England) and in every sphere of life, from child rearing (Johann Heinrich Pestalozzi) to "Aesthetic Families"—and manifest in the imagery of laissez-faire through which he presents utopia: everyman his own universe, minimal government, and "Uniters . . . absolutely isolated." So considered, the drama in the journal entries centers on a far-reaching ideological conflict. Emerson's endorsement of the socialists' goals stems from his belief in individuality; his attraction to an ideal individualism stems from his prior, deeper commitment to his culture. The gap in the journal entry suggests that he had not resolved the conflict by 1842. More accurately, he had mystified its contradictions through the paradox of America. His early writings distinguish between Jacksonian society and the "true America," as between ideology and utopia. He criticizes the defects of laissez-faire in the name of "the Spirit of America" (to which he dedicated his journals in 1822, at the age of nineteen). He retreats from the pressures of specialization and industrialization, as well as from his private griefs, into "this new yet unapproachable America I have found in the West." "The American Scholar" opposes the prospect of "a nation of men" in America to America's "iron-lid[ded]" marketplace economy.[12] Upon such distinctions—grounded in an absolute that gains substance from the metaphors of the American way while, paradoxically, transcending the actual way itself by rhetorical inversion, opposition, and reversal—Emerson built his radical vision of the individual. America was for him alternately the facts of "actual individualism" and the ideal of spiritual fulfillment, a state of symbolic tension that appeared sometimes as sheer antagonism, sometimes as probational conflict, and whose divergent meanings Emerson embodied in his consummate figure of dissent, the representative/adversarial American Self.

The complexities of that figure are also those of Hester's sainted individualism. Essentially, Emerson shared the radical skepticism about institutions that Hester voices midway through the novel; he shared the same outrage at the abuses of political office and the ravages of social anomie that Hawthorne details in "The Custom-House." "There is nothing of the true democratic element in what is called [American] Democracy; it must fall, being wholly commercial": this in 1836, the year before "The American Scholar." Four years later, just before the publication of *Essays: First Series,* he wrote: "I see that commerce, law, & state employments . . . are now all so perverted & corrupt that no man can right himself in them. . . . Nothing is left him but to begin the world anew." What Emerson meant by beginning the world anew devolved then and always upon the "radical doctrine of the individual," "the doctrine Judge for yourself[,] Reverence thyself." But at that point self-reverence had assumed such absolutist proportions in his thought, had brought him so close to a relativistic view of the merely social order, that, like the radical Hester, he actually entertained the possibility of a wholesale reordering of the state. In his lectures, journals, and letters of 1840–41 he comes *to the verge* of advocating the redistribution of property and wealth and sometimes *seems* to venture further still, *almost* beyond the bounds of liberalism:

All our fanatics high & low seem to move now impelled by ideas which may one day emerge to the surface under the form of the question of Property. Every child that is born ought to have his just chance—perhaps that is the statement that will content all.

The monastery[,] the convent did not quite fail. . . . The Society of Shakers did not quite fail. . . . The College has been dear to many an old bachelor of learning. What hinders that this Age better advised should endeavor to sift out these experiments the false & adopt & embody in a new form the advantage[?] . . . So say I of Brook Farm, Let it live. Its merit is that it is a new life. Why should we have only two or three ways of life & not thousands & millions?

The revolutions that impend over society are not now from ambition and rapacity, . . . but from new modes of thinking . . . which shall animate labor by love and science, which shall destroy the value of many kinds of property and replace all property within the dominion of reason and equity.[13]

I emphasize the qualifying terms—*almost, to the verge, seems*—because, of course, Emerson never really gave serious thought to social reorganization.* This is evident in the very

*Much the same can be said of Hawthorne, even in his Brook Farm days. As George Eliot pointed out in her 1852 review of *The Blithedale Romance* (in *The Recognition of Nathaniel Hawthorne,* ed. Benjamin Bernard Cohen [Ann Arbor: University of Michigan Press, 1969], 67):

Take the moral of Zenobia's history, and you will find that Socialism is apparently made responsible for consequences which it utterly condemned, and tried, at least, to remedy. We say, apparently, for it is really not made responsible for anything, good, bad, or indifferent. It forms a circumference of circumstances, which neither mould the characters, nor influence the destinies, of the individuals so equivocally situated,—forms,

playfulness of his language ("good fanatics," "will content all," "did not quite fail") as well as in his shortlist of exemplary radicals (monks, nuns, Shakers, and the old bachelor professor). Even at the height of his heresy (1836–41)—especially perhaps at that optative-utopian moment—he could not take seriously the "experiments" in collective living and common wealth. Even as his revulsion against Jacksonian free enterprise carried him to the edge of a Nietzschean contempt for democracy, an antagonism to "actual union" (North and South) that bordered on Romantic titanism, his vision of America proved a barrier to the antiliberal thrust of individuality—rhetorically and conceptually, a taboo against the extremes of hero worship, spiritual aristocracy, and organic hierarchy. Emerson nowhere more clearly reveals the impress of the symbology he inherited than in his most visionary flights of self-reliance. The more virulent his attacks on American society, the more firmly he grounds his radicalism in what can only be called the liberal millennium, whether as a purified version of free enterprise (as in the 1842 journal) or, more familiarly, as a pastoral dream of agrarian laissez-faire.

Hence the significance of his confrontation with socialism. It was neither its theory nor its practice that really engaged Emerson but, rather, what these implied about his own visionary commitments. In such implications—not in programs for collectivist living, not in the affirmation of collectivist princi-

in short, not an essential part of the picture, but an enormous fancy border, not very suitable for the purpose for which it was designed. Zenobia's life would have been exhibited with more propriety, and its moral brought home with more effect, in the "theatre" of the world, out of which it really grew, and of which it would have formed a vital and harmonious part. . . . Zenobia and Socialism should have been acted in the ready-made theatre of ordinary humanity, to see how it would fare with them there. Having occupied the ground, Hawthorne owed it to truth, and to a fit opportunity, so to dramatize his experience and observation of Communistic life, as to make them of practical value for the world at large.

ples, not in the critique of individualism or its exaggerations, but in the denial of the Spirit of America—lay the challenge of socialism. What compelled Emerson's interest in this regard was his recognition of a different road to utopia, an alternative model of culture. Socialism repudiated the very rhetoric of America; it contested the concept itself of the United States as the country of the future. As method and in theory, socialism rejected the ironies of American historiography together with the ambiguities of group pluralism. It denied the newness of the New World (as against the outwornness of the Old); denied the legend of the Puritan founders, the myth of the American Revolution, the claims of manifest destiny, and the typology of the open, regenerative West. In short, socialism tended toward a total, unequivocal dissociation of the ideal not only from the United States but also from the meaning of America.

And by 1842 Emerson had to acknowledge the seriousness of the challenge. Too many others were taking it up, including the young transcendentalists he names in the 1842 journal entry; he was being solicited by intimates for support of Brook Farm; and he was being deluged, he complained, by radical tracts and manifestoes in which, astutely, he read the signs of impending revolution in Europe.* The result was the cultural-rhetorical

*The Concord discussion groups of these years provide an interesting index to Emerson's confrontation with socialist doctrines. One example must suffice here, a "Convention at Alcott-House"—reported by Emerson in October—which took as its subject the radical proposal, advanced by various European socialists, "that an integral reform will comprise . . . an emendment in our (1) Corn Laws, (2) Monetary Arrangements, (3) Penal Code, (4) Education, (5) the Church, (6) the Law of Primogeniture, (7) Divorce" (*Dial* 3 [1842]: 242–47). The sweep of overturnings is worthy of Hester at her most speculative, and the response, which Emerson endorses, indicates the principles that guided both him and Hawthorne (albeit in different ways and to different ends) through their encounters with collectivist utopianism. The argument develops in three stages. The Protestant-liberal response, which moves from a Weberian harmony of secular and sacred concerns to a threatening friction between pluralist rule by law and the spirit of universal love:

> a personal reform . . . is obviously the key to every future and wider good. By reformed individuals only can reformed laws be enacted, or reformed

crisis I noted; its issue has been hinted at. Increasingly through the 1840s, Emerson drew out the liberal underpinnings of his dissent—which is to say, the premises of his commitment to America in its full ambiguity, ideal and (not or) actual. And, increasingly through the decade, he engaged in a pointed, persistent, and eventually vehement polemic against socialism. Having discovered that he "could not reconcile the socialist principle with [his] own doctrine of the individual," he proceeded to situate individuality within culture, as individualism.[14]

> plans effected. By him alone, who is reformed and well regulated, can the appeal fairly be made to others, either privately or publicly. . . . Personal elevation is our credentials. . . .
>
> After this had been considered and approved, another of our friends offered the following [query:] . . . "How shall we find bread for support of our bodies?" . . . And the government's answer was immediately proffered, "We . . . shield the good from adversities, and we punish the evildoers." Is this true? We thought. . . . No; government had not redeemed its promise to us, and we would no longer care for its provisions. The first law, too, of Heaven is Love, and government is founded on force. . . .
>
> We, therefore, ignore human governments . . . and declare our allegiance only to Universal Love.

At this critical juncture, where laissez-faire threatens to slip into antinomianism, a "third person" offers the following thought, based on the text from Revelation, "Behold I make all things new": "the germs of this new generation are even now discoverable in human beings, but have been hitherto either choked by uncongenial circumstances, or . . . have attained no abiding growth." And from this utopian perspective, the discussion finds its resolution by descending from theory to "method," or, more precisely, by investing the "Universal" in local process:

> On a survey of the present civilized world, Providence seems to have ordained the United States of America, more especially New England, as the field wherein this idea is to be realized in actual experience. . . .
>
> An unvitiated generation and more genial habits shall restore the Eden on Earth, and men shall find that paradise is not merely a fable of the poets.
>
> Such was the current of our thought; and most of those who were present felt delight in the conversations that followed. Said I not well, that it was a happy day? For though talk is never more than a portraiture of a fact, it may be, and ours was, the delineation of a fact based in the being of God.

The 1842 lacuna marks Emerson's presentiment of the relation in his thought between ideology and utopia. The direct acknowledgment of that bond is first recorded in "New England Reformers" (March, 1844), an eloquent summary of his ruminations over the past four years about socialism. In 1842, soon after Brook Farm got under way, he wrote privately that the socialists "had skipped no fact but one, namely, life." Subsequent events seemed to have confirmed his judgment, among them the deterioration of Brook Farm, as he saw it, into "the center of Fourierism in the United States." As Hawthorne put it (through the divergent views of Coverdale and Zenobia in *The Blithedale Romance*), that motley group of idealists—"Persons of marked individuality . . . [whose] bond was not affirmative, but negative"—had "blundered into the very emptiest mockery [of an] . . . effort to establish the one true system." Emerson was provoked by such blunders to a more or less systematic attack against reformers at home and abroad. To all varieties of ultraists he offers a general rebuke (one that the radical Hester can be said to embody at the novel's end) concerning the primacy of the self:

> The criticism and attack on institutions . . . which we have witnessed [against everything from "the system of agriculture" to "the institution of marriage"] has made one thing plain, that society gains nothing whilst a man, not himself renovated, attempts to renovate things around him.

Then Emerson proceeds to his own visionary alternative. Lifting virtually verbatim the long journal passage of 1842, he hails the current "spirit of protest" (a world "awakening to the idea of union") and repeats its many "magic" effects, from communication "by lightning" to "concert" without words. He omits only the separation of fact from ideal ("It is spiritual and must not be actualized") and makes only one addition, as though to explain why that separation no longer obtains. What had been, amorphously, "union ideal,—in actual individualism, actual union" is rendered, apodictically, "The union must be ideal, in actual individualism."[15]

Actual individualism, ideal union! The paradox is ultimately Christic, the incarnation applied to a secular way of life. It is a rhetorical flourish adequate to the occasion, Emerson's first public use of the word "individualism." He does not consciously acquiesce to ideology. By "actual," he means a version of the ideal (though always, tellingly, by contrast with socialism). And yet through this same decade the ideological tenets of Emersonian individualism become increasingly clear. The contours of the free enterprise paradise that were shadowed forth in 1842 are detailed in the frequent and direct "correspondences"—reiterated throughout Emerson's writings after 1844—"between the concept of laissez-faire and the natural world," as propounded by Adam Smith, the only "great man among the economists."[16] And the correspondences themselves are increasingly grounded in a sweeping ideological distinction. Socialism had the idea but the reverse methods; liberalism too had the idea, and, in addition, it had the means and methods to realize it. As an idea, individualism had been the dream of all ages, but not all ages, Emerson now realized, were the same. The gospel of Christ had made a difference, as had Plato's Athens and now, in this modern period, the discovery of America. With the War of Independence "another hour had struck, other forms arose," and a new principle of "actual union" had been set loose on the world, a "moral credo" comparable to Newton's *principia:* "Gravity is the Laissez faire principle, or Destiny, or Optimism, than which nothing is wiser or stronger."[17]

So perceived, history unfolded in a threefold spiral from East to West, Athens to Jerusalem, and Rome toward America, land of "the Modern." Here, where "commerce . . . science, [and] philosophy" were at last keeping pace, and where "the laws of nature play through trade," a new idea had come to light: "the individual is the world. This perception is a sword such as was never drawn before." Now, "for the first time," the dream of self-reliance was organic to a certain society, in a certain place, as a tendency toward perfect union inherent in its laws, customs, assumptions, and institutions. Emerson set out this vision in "The Young American," an address delivered in February, 1844, a month before "New England Reformers" and equally influenced, according to recent scholarship, by his conversations with Hawthorne. It might be read as the liberal-Romantic version of Dimmesdale's election day jeremiad. Where Dimmesdale had spoken of a wilderness to be planted, Emerson invokes "the *land* . . . itself," this "bountiful continent [that] is ours, state on state, and territory on territory, to the waves of the Pacific." Where Dimmesdale reached back for authority to "the old prophets of Israel" (332), Emerson points to "the new and anti-feudal power of Commerce," including the railroad, open markets, and free trade, whose history is the "sublime and friendly Destiny by which the human race is guided." This history, he announces, has already made New England the country's "leader" and will make America the "leading nation" of the world: "One thing is plain for all men of common sense and common conscience, that here, here in America, is the home of man."[18]

It amounts to a breathtaking work of culture—a wholesale appropriation of utopia, all the hopes of reform and revolution nourished on both sides of the Atlantic by the turmoil of modernization, for the American Way. From that Young American perspective, Emerson repudiated the European Forty-eight. What vitiated the revolutions abroad, he decided, during his travels that year to London and Paris, was their antipathy to the "doctrine of the individual." It was not so much the violence that troubled him. As a utopianist, he could accommodate ideas of all kinds, including insurrection under extreme circumstances. He demanded only that insurrection serve the cause of utopia as he defined it. And in 1848 he discovered experientially what he had worked out years before in his journals and lectures, that cause, means, and method were inseparable from actual individualism. For Emerson the European revolutions were not a test but the confirmation of basic convictions. This view accounts for the generosity of his response. His sympathy for the "mobs" of Paris and London, "dragged in their ignorance by furious chiefs to the Red Revolution," was grounded in his now-firm belief that all hope for change, reformist or revolutionary, belonged to individualism:

> Individualism has never been tried. All history[,] all poetry deal with it only, & because now it was in the minds of men to go alone and now before it was tried, now, when a few began to think of the celestial Enterprise, sounds this tin trumpet of a French Phalanstery and the newsboys throw up their caps & cry, Egotism is exploded; now for Communism! But all that is valuable in the Phalanstery comes of individualism.

The sense of repose we feel in this conjunction of "celestial" union and actual "Enterprise" is contextualized for us at midcentury by Emerson's overview of the modern options for radical change: on the one hand, "revolutions . . . in the interest of feudalism and barbarism," such as those he had just witnessed in Europe; on the other hand, "revolutions in the interest of society," culminating in "the planting of America." The Atlantic Ocean, he wrote, describing his 1848 ocean crossing from the Old World back to the New, "is a sieve through which only or chiefly the liberal[,] adventurous[,] sensitive[,] *America-loving* part of each city, clan, family, are brought . . . [and] the Europe of Europe is left."[19]

This is not the spirit in which Hester Prynne returns, and it is almost the reverse of that in which she discards the A midway through the novel. But the Emersonian parallel helps explain the nature of her appeal in both cases. It reminds us, to begin with, that the symbol of dissent is not her act of discarding the letter. It is the discarded letter itself, the "jewel" that is "lost" so that it may be redeemed, although (or because) its redemption invests it, potentially, with a radical resistance to closure. The act of discarding is a partial truth, one side of symbolic polarity that is processually resolved: first, in the forest by Pearl; then, by Hester when she returns; then, by Hawthorne in the customshouse; and repeatedly through the novel, by the opposition between author and narrator as it is transmuted into complementarity through Hawthorne's directives for interpretation. But, considered in and for itself, the "embroidered letter" at the water's edge, "a hand's breadth" away from oblivion, points us in a different direction. Never does the A more vibrantly represent the imperatives of whim, free will, defiance, and abandonment, and never does it more sternly recall us to the fact that its office has not yet been done. It stands for the paradox of autonomy preserved, precariously but decisively, and all the more decisively for its precariousness within the bounds of culture.

The journal entries of November/December 1842 may be said to have launched Emerson, fresh from his "heretical," "antinomian"* *Essays: First Series,* on a journey from utopia to

*"Heretical" is a term applied to Emerson's early work by his Unitarian elders, though subsequently, of course, Emerson became a patron saint of Unitarianism. "Antinomian" is a more complex application, but it seems clear that the scholarly tradition that identifies Emerson with antinomianism is clearly mistaken in any technical sense of the term. Emerson himself makes this explicit (e.g., *Journals,* ed. William G. Gilman [Cambridge, Mass.: Harvard University Press, 1960–75], 5:495–96), and various scholars have elaborated on the distinctions, most recently Ivy Schweitzer, "Transcendental Sacramentals: 'The Lord's Supper' and Emerson's Doctrine of Form," *New England Quarterly* 61 (1988): 410–18. Some of them, indeed, find Emerson to be close to "Orthodox Puritan concepts of the spirit" (Wesley T. Mott, "Emerson and Antinomianism: The Legacy of the Sermons," *American Literature* 1 [1978]: 369–96), and, I would add, particularly close to the concepts of preparation formulated by his seventeenth-century immigrant progenitor Peter Bulkeley (who also influenced Jonathan Edwards). Nonetheless, the dissent of the early essays can be said to evoke the specter of antinomianism, as Hester Prynne does, at the boundaries of "America" (but within them) and on behalf of individualism. It would make for an interesting comparative culture study to contrast *Essays: First Series* with another essay collection of the

ideology, but the relation between those two sites is dynamic, not linear, and the journey from one to the other is not so much a progression, or regression, as it is an oscillation between center and circumference. The European Forty-eight marks the return of Emerson's utopia to its ideological home. Emerson's early (and abiding) utopianism demonstrates the radical energies potential in liberal ideology. The same convictions that led him to reject socialism also impelled him a decade earlier outward to the revolutionary concepts of European individuality. It was not then, or ever, a matter of transcending his culture, but, on the contrary, of plumbing its depths, carrying its basic premises as far as they would go, to the rim of the ideologically conceivable—the frontiers and/or boundaries of consensus—and thereby, paradoxically, drawing out (amplifying, heightening, universalizing) the grounds of consensus in the act of challenging the culture. The later essays collapse that paradox into ambiguity. They also indicate by contrast the enabling source of paradox. Emersonian dissent reminds us that ideology in America requires a constant conflict between self and society: the self in itself, a separate, single, resistant individuality; and society en masse, individualism systematized. And it reminds us that the utopian imperative requires us to interpret individuality within the ideological boundaries of actual individualism.

These are also the contradictory-reconciliatory terms of "America": a cultural symbol built on the gap-to-be-bridged between individual and society. The process of bridging, we have seen, is inextricably adversarial and integrative. As "America," it compels the opposition between the actual and the

same year, Pierre Leroux's *Sept discours sur la situation actuelle de la société et de l'esprit humain* (Paris: 1841), including the discourse "On Individualism and Socialism," which Leroux addresses in emphatically non-Emersonian fashion, "Aux Bourgeois et aux Prolétaires"; the collection as a whole takes as its motto the biblical injunction "We seek the city of the future."

ideal; as oppositionalism, it binds conflict itself to the categories of individual and society. In a sense, these categories are archetypal, universal (as are virtually all other ideological categories, including those of slave and feudal societies), but here as elsewhere they gather substance from their specific historical content. "America" identifies the archetype in terms of a certain modern community that is universal and national ("the nation of futurity") and then represents this community through a certain concept of subjectivity (democratic, independent, and self-made) that is universal and cultural. Emersonian self-reliance identifies dissent as the quintessentially American gesture and then universalizes it as the radical imperative to subjectivity. From either perspective, the gap-to-be-bridged elicits our opposition by providing a barrier to the wrong kind of process—the kind, for example, that would "reduce" dissent to the "merely social" terms of race, class, or gender. Or in positive terms, it directs our opposition toward American dissent by translating such categories as race, class, and gender as social "limitations," to be transcended en route to representative individualism, a sainted subjectivity of one's own, like Hester's prophecy of the ideal woman actualized in her own penitence *to be.*

"Civil society," writes Jürgen Habermas, describing the basis of liberal cohesion, is

> conceived as a principle of marketlike . . . association. For [in Hegel's words] "the principle of modern states has prodigious strength and depth because it allows the principle of subjectivity to progress to its culmination in the extreme of self-subsistent personal particularity, and yet at the same time brings it back to the substantive unity and so maintains this unity in the principle of subjectivity itself."

Habermas offers this account as the modern "solution" to "the problem of mediation of state and society."[20] But the solution itself rests on a paradoxical "and yet"—which is to say, it not only allows but calls for a continuing dissonance between unity and subjectivity. Translated into the terms of pluralist interpretation, these dynamics issue in *The Scarlet Letter* in the discrepancy between the narrator's view of Hester's self-reliance and ours, an opposition to be mediated intersubjectively through the office of the reader. Hawthorne's directives for interpretation serve in this respect to control subjectivity, but, in doing so, they elicit the volatile energies potential in individualism, a utopian force encoded in the liberal process itself. Like the discarded A at the margins of community, it makes for a form of protest that is bound to challenge the consensus it represents—*bound* to challenge and thereby authorized by the culture to sustain the polarity of self and society upon which consensus paradoxically depends.

Let me reiterate that the issue here is neither Hawthorne's radicalism nor his debt to Emerson. It is Hester's *sainted* individualism, a central and persistent response to the novel that Hawthorne evokes (within the novel itself as well as in the reader) as one of several clues to interpretation. His own dissent was always hedged, even during his Brook Farm idyll, by a conservatism far beyond Emerson's, even in Emerson's complacent later writings. We might say of both men that they gave expression to certain volatile forces that erupted at mid-century under the pressures of massive social change. But volatility and change, we know, may become agents of integration. This in fact describes Hawthorne's use of irony and ambiguity, as it does Emerson's 1844 vision of the ideal actualized, processually, in individualism. And yet that vision, like Hawthorne's strategy of negation, posits a perpetual tension between means and ends—continually forces a gap between process and closure, where closure means repose in the values of liberal culture, where process builds on the appeal to the volatile utopianism of individuality, and where volatility itself is at once a form of opposition and a function of social context, like the wild rosebush in Hawthorne's novel set against the prison door.

So considered, the difference between the two writers recalls the pervasive cultural tensions at mid-century between expansion and consolidation. Emerson's radical individualism (1836–41) invests the self with the boundlessness of free enterprise capitalism in an apparently open, empty, and endlessly malleable New World. The paradoxes it contains are famously compressed in John Jay Chapman's apostrophe to transcendentalist No-saying: "If a soul be taken and crushed by democracy till it utter a cry, that cry will be Emerson" (and then the broader explanation: "While the radicals of Europe were revolting in 1848 against the abuses of a tyranny whose roots were in feudalism, Emerson, the great radical of America, the arch-radical of the world, was . . . bringing back the attention of political thinkers to its starting point, the value of human character," or individualism). In our own time, they find their amplest commentary in the Emersonian polemics left and right concerning "the culture of narcissism" at one extreme; at another, "the current flight from individuality in literary critical circles"; and, at the philosophical center, Stanley Cavell's recuperation of Emersonian "aversion" as a perennial mediation between individuality and individualism, self-reliance and conformity, on behalf of a radically American mode of consent. *The Scarlet Letter* expresses the pressures toward reaggregation at a moment of deep cultural anxiety (1848–52). It finds its amplest commentary in those critics who, following the logic of Hester's return, teach us how to have our dissent and do the work of society, too. Its single best New Critical gloss is Charles Feidelson's analysis of Hester's penitence "yet to be," which "will always be unfinished" because it involves "a perennial conversion of the stuff of sin and sorrow into positive freedom—the creativity, individuality, and sympathetic community of natural men."[21]

Hawthorne, we might say, conveys the special genius of liberal culture in staging interpretation as a drama of dissent. Emerson demonstrates how the same visionary appeal that restricts dissent within the bounds of the American ideology may also turn "America"—rhetorically and, hence, morally and politically—into an ideological battleground.* It is a battleground of the margins, externally defined by the symbolic American frontier and internally by the potentiality embodied in the representative American. Richard Poirier calls this the area of "resistance in itself." "Whenever an arrangement," he writes, meaning any form of social aggregation, "threatens to hem in life, [Emerson] recommends 'abandonment,'" and Poirier links abandonment in this sense persuasively to William James's pragmatism:

the universe has always appeared to the natural mind as a kind of enigma, of which the key must be sought in the shape of some illuminating or power-bringing word or name. That word names the universe's *principle,* and to possess it is, after a fashion, to possess the universe itself. "God," "Matter," "Reason," "the Absolute," "Energy," are so many solving names. You can rest when you have them. You are at the end of your metaphysical quest.

But if you follow the pragmatic method, you cannot look on any such word as a closing your quest. You must bring out of each word its practical cash-value, set it as work within the stream of your experience. It appears less as a solution, then, than as a program for more work, and more particularly as an indication of the ways in which existing realities may be *changed.*[22]

*Emerson's use of "America" in this regard involves a paradox implicit in "the ironies of A-history" (chapter 2)—namely, that the revolution that identified the United States with independence and newness also instated the American Puritan legacy. The continuities thus established were rhetorical, a clear case of the invention of tradition. But, as rhetoric, they served a contradictory double function. On one hand, they expressed a basic conservatism; on the other hand, they sanctioned (as traditional) a certain radical impulse. It was an invention that absorbed the very concept of revolution into the meaning of America while empowering America with a revolutionary imperative. These cultural bivalences played an important role in Emerson's response to European socialism. In a separate study I examine that response in its larger transatlantic context, including the contrast between the American and French revolutions, the failure in France of revolutionary strategies of containment, and the difference from this perspective between the utopian speculators of Jacksonian America and the totalistic, schematic transformations advanced by reformers such as Charles Fourier and Claude Henri de Rouvroy Saint-Simon.

I cite this radical Emersonian connection because of the contrast it offers in tone and substance to the pragmatics of *The Scarlet Letter*. Hawthorne makes it the office of his narrator precisely to recommend *against* Hester's impulse to abandon and, after her return, to enclose her still-resisting self in history and community. And no doubt that office to some significant extent expresses his own consciously anti-Emersonian understanding (in 1848–52) of "the ways in which existing realities may be *changed*." For Hawthorne, as for his narrator, the issue is not stasis or change but whether change shall overturn or conserve, and in the end both Hawthorne and his narrator require us to leave the system intact, as Hester does—radically *un*changed, except in rhetoric and vision.

As rhetoric and vision, however, the novel opens through our interpretation to the paradoxes of dissent. The contrast I spoke of between Emerson and Hawthorne is also a radical complementarity: it suggests the capacities of culture to shape the subversive in its own image and thereby, within limits, to be shaped in turn by the radicalism it seeks to contain. Theodore Adorno claims (as the summa of "negative dialectics") that to be radical is not to "bow to *any* alternatives," since "freedom means to criticize and change situations, not to confirm by deciding within their coercive structure." Hester's sainted individualism and Emersonian self-reliance testify against that Marxist-aesthetic dream of autonomy. Or to put it in positive terms, they testify to the oppositional forms generated within the structures of society—in Hawthorne's terms, somewhere at the hither verge of cultural coercion; or, in Emerson's, at some transitional moving point, perpetually inchoate because transitional on principle, between center and circumference. If the abandoned A ambiguously ensures Hester's return, her return ironically vindicates her gesture of abandonment. Both moments—at the brook's edge (boundary of the liminal) and at her cottage threshold (frontier of reaggregation)—have the consecration of Emersonian paradox as recorded, for instance, in his journals of late November or early December, 1842, alongside his first remarks on the meaning of individualism:

> Self help is good, & is very much applauded by the bystanders, but there are better things than self help,—abandonment, for example, to the great spirit, without hurry to do or to be anything,—content with saying, "It is good to be here."[23]

Dissent in America is neither a mode of co-optation nor a force for subversion, though it may tend toward the integration of adversarial impulses or toward continuing resistance, including recurrent demands for social change. In either case, it is the expression of a particular utopian consciousness developed within the premises of liberal culture. It carries the profoundly destabilizing energies released by that culture in its formative phase (well designated "the era of boundlessness")[24] and it sustains that profoundly energizing, centrifugal thrust by an appeal to individuality (as subjectivity) as the sine qua non of union, an appeal expressed in *The Scarlet Letter* through the dynamics of interpretation and grounded, as Emerson's 1842 journal demonstrates, in the combined sacred and secular authority of Protestant nonconformity and the theory of natural rights. These liberal premises provided an effective framework for social cohesion before the Civil War and, after it, a triumphant rhetoric of regional and continental incorporation. They also generated the enormous volatility that on the one hand fueled civil war and on the other hand allowed for the infusion of individuality into the very concept of nationhood. So circumscribed and so empowered, the paradoxes of dissent constitute a distinctive type of radical thought, at once opposed to systemic individualism and dependent on it—a radicalism as compelling in its way, and as comprehensive, as the competing socialist types of radical consciousness then emerging in Europe.

The distinction I would make here requires a word of explanation. Recently, the subversive in literature has been raised to the transcendent status once reserved for the noble, the tragic, and the complex. The result is a familiar allegory with a new twist: a Manichaean struggle between the One and the Many (as between good and evil) in which the One takes the antagonist guise of Heterogeneity. Every hegemony, we are told, is hegemonic in its own way, but all forms of subversion, like all happy families, are essentially alike. My assumption is that oppositional forms, like those of cohesion, co-optation, and incorporation, are fundamentally and variously forms of culture. "Emergent," "residual," "antihegemonic," "utopian"–all such definitions of the subversive are useful insofar as we demystify their essentialist claims to universality and the Real. The same applies to the many anti-individualistic movements that coalesced in the European Forty-eight, collectivism in all its varieties ("the Phalanx, owenism, Simonism, the Communities"). It applies as well to Hester's sainted individualism, a mode of resistance on our part that is especially susceptible both to liberal strategies of socialization and to the ideals of radical individuality.

Hence the vibrant oppositional force of the discarded A in *The Scarlet Letter.* Early in the novel Hawthorne tells us that under the burden of the A Hester seemed to be "giving up her individuality . . . [and to] become the general symbol . . . of woman's frailty and sinful passion" (185). But, of course, the case is just the reverse. Hester's individuality emerges through her capacity to make the general symbol her own, an act of appropriation through dissent whose office is fulfilled at the end, when she returns to New England accompanied both by rumors of Pearl in Europe and by hopes of better things in store for America. That liberal both/and includes an alternative either/or: the concept of an un-American place of freedom, Europe; the possibility of an American nonliberal future, some still undetermined "surer ground of mutual happiness" whose structures will contravene those of actual individualism.

Such alternatives, however—*un*-American, *anti*- or *non*liberal—are included (like Pearl's aristocratic foreign marriage) mainly for symbolic contrast. They constitute an adversarial prefix hinging on a certain dominant culture; a frontier forbidding trespass, like the Ur-lintel of Passover, the scarlet symbol that forbade access to the dwellings of the chosen people. But within the chosen boundaries of that symbology, they function to open frontiers and create access. As the ideological marks of the unthinkable (un-American, anti- or nonliberal), they set out by contrast the ideological prospects for dissent, the grounds for a resistant subjectivity that is potentially (for us if not for Hawthorne or even Hester) the source of radical insight and social change.

Anthropologically considered, this is liminality extended into a way of life, antistructure reconceived as a vehicle of progress.* It has all the energy of pure utopia—of an ideal (to recall the phrase Emerson deleted in 1844) that "must not be actualized"—but with a certain liberal difference. At its most intense, writes Hans Blumenberg, utopia is "a sum of negations": it avoids "contamination by what currently exists" by banning all definition whatever, placing "a prohibition against saying anything positively imagined . . . about the new land as it will be."[25] That prohibition is encoded in the office of the A, except that here it also expresses something already imagined: the new land as America; ideal union in actual individualism;

*Recent anthropologists have argued cogently that the traditional model of the ritual process, leading from liminality to reaggregation, emphasizes mechanisms of control as opposed to agencies of change—that it tends toward a conservative, ultimately static dichotomy between culture and chaos. At times, however, the new ethnography seems to instate an equally static dichotomy between repressive structure and critical marginality. I refer to the various current "oppositional" polarities in literary as well as anthropological studies, in which an earlier dream of timeless tribal harmony (the modernist nostalgia for order and *communitas*) is replaced by something like its rhetorical opposite—the dream of pervasive subversion, an academic nostalgia for radical agency that in some cases borders on an essentialism (and a transcendence) of its own.

and the letter of prophecy empowered by the spirit of abandonment. In short, it also expresses the radicalism latent in the interstices of free enterprise theory, the gaps or lacunae potential in the principle of subjectivity itself. So interpreted, the scarlet letter is an adversarial representation of cultural process, whose radical office lies in its capacity to be nourished by the structures it resists—among these, the rhetorical structures of actual individualism, whereby "each man," as Emerson wrote skeptically in "The Young American," "may find what he wishes to buy, and expose what he has to sell," and "where all human wishes," as Hawthorne put it ironically in "The Intelligence Office," "may be negotiated to their fulfillment."

Postscript

I HAVE BEEN arguing that text and context are reciprocal: that to understand *The Scarlet Letter* in its own terms is not only to see the ideological dimensions of its art but also to bring into view the enormous imaginative resources of mid-nineteenth-century American liberalism. My assumption throughout has been that ideological analysis can be a richly aesthetic form of criticism. Properly conceived, I believe, it is an approach that blends the appreciative and the cognitive, and which tends in doing so to replace the reductive polarities of both old formalisms and new moralisms—universal or parochial, transcendent or political, subversive or conventional—with a more flexible sense of the interactive elements in art as cultural work. Such considerations have kept my reading of *The Scarlet Letter* within the boundaries of Hawthorne's interpretive framework. Still, ideological analysis assumes a priori that such boundaries are limited by history, and since that assumption constitutes the adversarial donnée of this essay—somewhat as the adultery prohibition serves as the novel's donnée—I would like in closing to take note of the limitations implicit in the office of the A. To that end I return one last time to the question of interpretation, but now from a position tangential (or perhaps, in Cavell's sense, aversive) to the directives that Hawthorne provides. So perceived, those directives seem a form of special pleading; their very insistence betrays an underlying cultural-authorial anxiety. Hawthorne intends his winding indirections to control interpretation, and they do. But the windings themselves made for what he privately called "a h – – l-f – – – d story." The repressed letters can be taken as one sign of a strain in his method. Another was his wife Sophia's splitting headache after he read the last chapter aloud to her. When she recovered, she wrote to her sister Mary: "I don't know what you will think of the Romance. It is most powerful and contains a moral as terrific & stunning as a thunderbolt. It shows that the Law cannot be broken."[1]

Surely, Sophia was not just thinking of the seventh commandment. She was reacting, I think, as Nathaniel was, to the enormous cultural pressures brought to bear upon the conclusion. "The scarlet letter had not done its office": the entire novel asks us to interpret this teleologically, in the affirmative, and by the end it compels us to, as a grim necessity. It is as though Hawthorne had to overcompensate for the enormous power of dissent potential in his characters and symbols, had to find some moral absolute – some equivalent in the liberal imagination for the Thou Shalt Not's delivered from Mount Sinai – compelling enough to recall all those unleashed energies of will, eros, and language back into the culture from which they arose and, in his view, to which they belonged. He found the solution in the act of mimesis that his novel simultaneously endorses and enacts. It was to represent the development of his culture – both positively, by our ironic assent to the almost-absent Revolution that connects the novel's twin time frames, and negatively, by our ambiguous rejection of the radical politics that Hester disavows in absentia – to set forth the workings of the American liberal ideology, so interpreted, as the iron link between culture, nature, and the self, "the Law [that] cannot be broken."

It is to Sophia's credit that she found the "moral as terrific &

stunning as a thunderbolt." And it is to Hawthorne's credit that he not only made full use of the symbolic system at his disposal but also had the integrity to indicate, if not the full costs involved, then at least some signs whereby those costs might be inferred: the coercive force, for example, of containment by consent, including the containment of the consenting, hellfired artist in liberal democracy, which forms an illicit bond, a sort of marginal consensus-in-dissent, between the secret Hawthorne and the hidden Hester. It is that secret narrator, I have suggested, who finally compels Hester to resume the A, on the grounds that the symbol is not only the culture's but her own, a badge both of legal process and of radical individualism. And his (unspoken) argument is manifest in a compelling act of irony and ambiguity that encloses the letter once and for all within the boundaries of our intersubjective interpretations. But that sense of compulsion (on his part and ours) adds a discordant note to Hawthorne's orchestration of pluralist points of view. It recalls the strangely intense, unresolved moment in the customshouse when he tries on the A, the emblem of radical creativity as cultural inheritance, and finds it too hot to handle. Ideology, according to a recent essay on liberal rule by law, is "the gunman . . . in our heads"; it is not that society holds a gun to your head, but that "the gun at your head *is* your head."[2] This is perhaps what Sophia had in mind when she called "the Law" stunning. It may also be what Hawthorne refers to when, speaking of the scarlet letter in the conclusion, he describes his own splitting headache: "We . . . would gladly, now that it has done its office, erase its deep print out of our own brain; where long meditation has fixed it in very undesirable distinctness" (340).

As a symbol for this and other unerased traces of contradiction in the novel—undesired silences that (again to Hawthorne's credit) do not quite succeed in silencing conflict—I should like to appropriate the "angry eagle" of "The Custom-House" for my own purposes, relocating it from "The Custom-House" of

1849 to the "War Matters" of 1862. In the later essay Hawthorne sought to reconcile himself with the consensus of another "iron age," and instinctively he returned once again to the myth of national origins:

> There is an historical circumstance, known to few, that connects the children of the Puritans with those Africans of Virginia in a very singular way. They are our brethren, as being lineal descendants of the Mayflower, the fated womb which in its first labor brought forth a brood of Pilgrims on Plymouth Rock, and, in a subsequent one, spawned slaves upon the Southern soil,—a monstrous birth, but one with which we have an instinctive sense of kindred, and so are stirred by an irresistible impulse to attend their rescue even at the cost of blood and ruin. The character of our sacred ship, I fear, may suffer a little by this revelation; but we must let her white progeny offset her dark one,—and two such portents never sprang from an identical source before.[3]

Hawthorne's *Mayflower* has all the major imaginative ingredients of the dominant culture: the legend of the Puritan theocracy, womb of American democracy; the ambiguities of good and evil, agency of compromise; and the ironies of regeneration through violence, rationale for civil war. But it is a symbol overdetermined by history. Its deeper meanings point insistently to the discontinuities of process and the precariousness of the hiatus that links "rescue" to "blood and ruin." The return of the *Mayflower* is a parable of social conflict following upon (as well as generating) cultural myth. It reverberates with multiple meanings at cross-purposes with each other: the recurrent American nightmare of miscegenation; the long literary procession of mutually destructive dark-white kin (from *Clotel* through *Clarel* and *Pudd'nhead Wilson* to *Absalom, Absalom!*); the biblical types of the elect and the damned (Seth and Ham, Jacob and Esau) through which the South defended its peculiar institution; the racist use of the image of Christic sacrifice through which the North sanctified the Union cause. Considered together with the "unhappy fowl," this "sacred ship" blackened by "revelation" is itself a monstrous birth, a Frankenstein's monster of the culture: history returning in the guise of figures designed to control it—the most familiar of symbols that now streams forth disjunctions, mocks the A-politics of both/and, and guides us, with an irony of its own, to the contradictions repressed by the novel's twin contexts, 1642–49 and 1848–52.

Let me conclude with that image, and underscore its peculiar volatility—structures of consensus founded upon the potential for dissent, rituals designed to consecrate the uncontained self, as in Kafka's parable of the leopards*—by recalling the image that Hester projects upon her return. First, then, Hawthorne's *Mayflower*-eagle, mother of nationhood and vixen of contradictions. Second, Hester come home, the dissenter as agent of socialization, a self-professed sinner self-transformed into a herald of progress. Two figures of ambiguity; two models of the relation between rhetoric and social action; two intersections between power and imagination; two tropes of the reciprocity between process and telos. They are opposites and yet uncannily alike, like the object and its reflection in a camera obscura—two sides of the same symbolic coin, representing the American ideology. *And* vice versa: they are alike and yet paradoxically disjunctive, two reflections of the American ideology whose contrasts point to the limitations of representation itself and so provide a different image of agency and process—a symbol of cultural work whose office has not been done.

*"Leopards break into the temple and drink the sacrificial chalices dry; this occurs repeatedly, again and again; finally it can be reckoned upon beforehand and becomes a part of the ceremony" ("Reflections," in *The Great Wall of China,* trans. Willa and Edwin Muir [New York: Schocken Books, 1960], 282). This ritual model must be supplemented, however, by a preceding reflection: "If it had been possible to build the Tower of Babel without ascending it, the work would have been permitted" (282).

Notes

Preface

1. Nathaniel Hawthorne, *The Scarlet Letter: A Romance,* in *Novels,* ed. Millicent Bell (New York: Library of America, 1983), 412; hereafter cited in text.

2. Sean Wilentz, "On Class and Politics in Jacksonian America," in *The Promise of American History: Progress and Prospects,* ed. Stanley I. Katler and Stanley N. Katz (Baltimore: Johns Hopkins University Press, 1982), 54–55; George Washington, *Writings,* ed. John C. Fitzpatrick (Washington, D.C.: U.S. Government Printing Office, 1940), 35: 219–20.

3. Herman Melville, "Hawthorne and His Mosses," in *The Piazza Tales and Other Prose Pieces 1839–1860*, ed. Harrison Hayford et al. (Evanston, Ill.: Newberry Library, 1987), 252; and *Pierre: or, The Ambiguities,* in *Pierre, Israel Potter, The Confidence-Man, Tales, and Billy Budd,* ed. Harrison Hayford (New York: Library of America, 1984), 286–99.

4. Theodore Lowi, *The End of Liberalism: The Second Republic of the United States* (New York: Norton, 1979); Michael Sandel, *Liberalism and the Limitations of Justice* (Cambridge: Cambridge University Press, 1982); Walt Whitman, "Song of Myself" (1855), in *Complete Poetry and Collected Prose,* ed. Justin Kaplan (New York: Library of America, 1982), 87.

5. Evert Duyckinck, review of *The Scarlet Letter,* in *Literary World* 6 (March 30, 1850): 324–25; Richard H. Brodhead, *The School of Hawthorne* (New York: Oxford University Press, 1986), 8–9, 51–52, 63.

6. Brodhead, *School of Hawthorne,* 53, 58–60, citing and summarizing nineteenth-century reviews.

7. Henry James, *Hawthorne,* in *Essays on Literature: American Writers, English Writers,* ed. Leon Edel (New York: Library of America, 1984), 319, 402–3, 319, 401.

Chapter One: The A-Politics of Ambiguity

1. Joseph Allen Boone, *Tradition Counter Tradition: Love and the Form of Fiction* (Chicago: University of Chicago Press, 1987), 48; Tony Tanner, *Adultery in the Novel: Contract and Transgression* (Baltimore: Johns Hopkins University Press, 1979), 13.

2. Amy S. Lang, *Prophetic Woman: Anne Hutchinson and the Problem of Dissent in the Literature of New England* (Berkeley: University of California Press, 1987), 58, 67.

3. Hawthorne, "The May-Pole of Merry Mount," in *Tales and Sketches,* ed. Roy Harvey Pearce (New York: Library of America, 1982), 370, 367, 363.

4. F. O. Matthiessen, *American Renaissance: Art and Expression in the Age of Emerson and Whitman* (New York: Oxford University Press, 1941), 276.

5. Frank Kermode, *The Classic: Literary Images of Permanence and Change* (New York: Knopf, 1975), 43.

6. Mikhail Bakhtin, *Problems in Dostoevsky's Poetics,* ed. and trans. Caryl Emerson (Minneapolis: University of Minnesota Press, 1984), passim; Hans Blumenberg, "The Concept of Reality and the Possibility of the Novel," in *New Perspectives in German Literary Criticism,* ed. Richard Amacher and Victor Lange (Princeton: Princeton University Press, 1979), 32.

7. Hawthorne, *Letters, 1843–1853* ed. Thomas Woodson, L. Neal Smith, and Norman Holmes Pearson, in *Works,* Centenary Edition (Columbus: Ohio State University Press, 1985), 16: 371.

8. Raymond Williams, *Marxism and Literature* (Oxford: Oxford University Press, 1977), 121–27.

9. T. Walter Herbert, Jr., "Nathaniel Hawthorne, Una Hawthorne, and *The Scarlet Letter:* Interactive Selfhoods and the Cultural Construction of Gender," *PMLA* 103 (1988): 285–97.

10. Francis Parkman, *The Jesuits in North America in the Seventeenth Century* (1867), in *France and England in North America,* ed. David Levin (New York: Library of America, 1983), 1: 343, 461, 466; Herman Melville, *The Confidence-Man: His Masquerade,* 994.

11. John Winthrop, *The History of New England,* ed. James Savage (Boston: Phelps and Farnham, 1825), 1:166; and "A Model of Christian Charity" (1630), in *Winthrop Papers,* ed. Stewart Mitchell (Boston: Massachusetts Historical Society, 1931), 2:124.

12. Alexis de Tocqueville, *Democracy in America,* ed. J. T. Mayer, trans. George Lawrence (Garden City, N.Y.: Doubleday, 1969), 72; Edwin Chapin, *The Relation of the Individual to the Republic* (Boston: Dutton and Wentworth, 1844), 27, 31.

Chapter Two: The Ironies of A-History

1. Hawthorne, "Endicott and the Red Cross," in *Tales and Sketches,* 548.

2. Hawthorne, "Oliver Cromwell," in *True Stories from History and Biog-*

raphy, ed. William Charvat et al., *Works*, Centenary Edition (Columbus: Ohio State University Press, 1980), 6:9–10, 47–48.

3. Ralph Waldo Emerson, "Wide World 12" (1824), in *The Journals and Miscellaneous Notebooks*, ed. William Gilman, Alfred Ferguson, and Merrell Davis (Cambridge, Mass.: Harvard University Press, 1961), 2:198; Anon., "America in 1846," *United States Magazine and Democratic Review* 18 (1846): 60–61.

4. George Bancroft, *History of the United States* (Boston: Little, Brown, 1856–74), 2:11, 23, 145–46, 16; 1:462–63; 6:450, 474; 1:313, 323; 8:474; 7:23, 21.

5. Hawthorne, *The House of the Seven Gables* and *The Marble Faun: Or, The Romance of Monte Beni*, in *Novels*, 425, 1238.

6. John Lothrop Motley, *Historic Progress and American Democracy* (New York: Scribners, 1869), 6; *Correspondence* (New York: Harper, 1889), 2:65 (letter to Oliver Wendell Holmes, February 26, 1862).

7. Motley, *Correspondence*, 2:62; Anon., "The Course of Civilization," *United States Magazine and Democratic Review* 6 (1839): 212; J. R. Williams, *Oration* (New Bedford, Mass.: J. G. W. Pope, 1835), 5; Richard Salter Storrs, "The Puritan Scheme of Natural Growth" (1857), in *New England Society Orations*, ed. Cephas Brainerd and Eveline Warner Brainerd (New York: Century, 1901), 2:333; Bancroft, *History*, 1:460–61; George Perkins Marsh, "Address" (1844), in *New England Society Orations*, 1:400.

8. Storrs, "Puritan Scheme," 332.

9. Storrs, "Puritan Scheme," 330, 333, 338; Marsh, "Address," 1:400; Jared Sparks, *Remarks on American History* (Boston: Tappin and Dennet, 1837), 17; Horace Bushnell, *The Fathers of New England* (1849; New York: Putnam, 1850), 7, 26–27, 9, 13.

10. Hawthorne, *Life of Franklin Pierce*, in *Tales, Sketches, and Other Papers*, in *Works*, Riverside Edition, ed. George Parsons Lathrop (Boston: Houghton Mifflin, 1883), 12:417.

11. Herbert, "Nathaniel Hawthorne," 297.

12. Hawthorne, "The Celestial Railroad," in *Tales and Sketches*, 808–25.

13. Anon., *The Salem Belle* (Boston: Tappin and Dennet, 1842), vii; John Adams, *Works*, ed. Charles Francis Adams (Boston: Little, Brown, 1856), 10:359; Convers Francis, *An Address* (Cambridge, Mass.: Hilyard and Brown, 1828), 5; Alice Spieseke, *The First Textbooks in American History* (New York: Teachers College of Columbia University, 1938), 128–30; Marcius Willson, *American History* (New York: Ivison and Phinney, 1856), 115; Samuel R. Hall and A. R. Baker, *School History of the United States* (Andover, Mass.: W. Pierce, 1839), 9–12; Michael Davitt Bell, *Hawthorne and the Historical Romance of New England* (Princeton: Princeton University Press, 1971), 24; C. Boynton, *Oration* (Cincinnati, Ohio: Tagart and Gardner, 1847), 8, 10–11.

14. Hawthorne, *Grandfather's Chair*, in *Works*, ed. Fredson Bowers, L. Neal Smith, and John Manning, Centenary Edition (Columbus: Ohio State University Press, 1972), 6:16, 40, 133.

15. John G. Palfrey, *History of New England* (Boston: Little, Brown, 1858),

1:618–23; Samuel E. Morrison, *Builders of the Bay Colony* (Boston: Houghton Mifflin, 1930), 93; Mark De Wolfe Howe and Louis F. Eaton, "The Supreme Judicial Power in the Colony of Massachusetts Bay," *New England Quarterly* 20 (1947): 291; Tocqueville, *Democracy*, 38, 39, 41, 43, 279. See also Laura Karobkin's forthcoming essay, "The Scarlet Letter of the Law: Hawthorne and Puritan Criminal Justice."

16. Tocqueville, *Democracy*, 177; Emerson, Journal E (1841), in *Journals*, ed. A. William Plumstead and Harrison Hayford (Cambridge, Mass.: Harvard University Press, 1969), 7:433, quoting Tocqueville, *Democracy in America*, trans. Henry Reeve (New York: Adlard and Saunders, 1838), 377–78.

17. Tocqueville, *Democracy*, 41–45.

18. Hawthorne, "Endicott," in *Tales and Sketches*, 543–44.

19. Bancroft, *History*, 1:275; William H. Prescott, *Memoranda*, ed. C. Harvey Gardiner (Norman: University of Oklahoma Press, 1961), 1:302; George Perkins Marsh, *The American Historical School: A Discourse* (Troy, N.Y.: J. C. Kneeland, 1847), 29; Sparks, *Remarks on American History*, 7; William Henry Channing, "The Judgment of Christendom," *The Spirit of the Age* 1 (1849): 265; John Williamson Nevin, "Human Freedom," *American Review* 7 (1848): 415–16; Bancroft, *History*, 2:454, 457; 4:152; 9:500; 10:78; 2:462.

20. John Cotton, *Exposition upon the Thirteenth Chapter of the Revelation* (London: Livewel, Chapman, 1655), 66; Samuel Danforth, *A Brief Recognition of New England's Errand into the Wilderness* (1671), in *The Wall and the Garden: Selected Massachusetts Election Sermons 1670–1775*, ed. A. William Plumstead (Minneapolis: University of Minnesota Press, 1968), 60; John Milton, *Areopagitica* (1644), ed. William Haller, in *Works*, ed. F. A. Patterson (New York: Columbia University Press, 1931), 4:341.

21. Bushnell, *Fathers of New England*, 14; Winthrop, "A Model of Christian Charity," in *Winthrop Papers*, 2:294; Danforth, *Errand*, 60.

22. John Cotton, *God's Promise to His Plantation* (1630), in *Old South Leaflets* (Boston: Directors of the Old South Works, 1896), 7 (53): 4.

23. Robert E. Ferguson, "'We Hold These Truths': Strategies of Control in the Literature of the Founders," in *Reconstructing American Literary History*, ed. Sacvan Bercovitch (Cambridge, Mass.: Harvard University Press, 1986), 1–22; Abraham Lincoln, *Collected Works*, ed. Roy P. Basler (New Brunswick, N.J.: Rutgers University Press, 1953), 1:112; 4:264; [O'Sullivan], "Great Nation of Futurity," *United States Magazine and Democratic Review* 6 (1839): 428–29, 427, 429.

24. William Prescott, "Bancroft's United States" (January, 1841), in *Biographical and Critical Miscellanies* (London: Lippincott, 1904), 1:297, 335, 290, 296; Bancroft, "The Necessity, the Reality, and the Promise of Progress of the Human Race" (1854); and "The Office of the People in Art, Government, and Religion" (1835), in *Literary and Historical Miscellanies* (New York: Harper, 1855), 492, 415, 425, 430, 431, 423.

25. Bancroft, *History*, 4:228–30; Martin Luther Hurlbut, *Oration*, 14, 13–14, 12; Herman Melville, *White-Jacket: or The World in a Man-of War*, in *Redburn*,

White-Jacket, Moby-Dick, ed. G. Thomas Tanselle (New York: Library of America, 1983), 505–6; and *Mardi and a Voyage Thither,* in *Typee, Omoo, Mardi,* ed. G. Thomas Tanselle (New York: Library of America, 1982), 1185.

26. Morton Horwitz, *The Transformation of American Law, 1780–1860* (Cambridge, Mass.: Harvard University Press, 1977); Rufus Choate, "The Importance of Illustrating New England History" (1833), in *Works,* ed. Samuel Gilman Brown (Boston: Little, Brown, 1862), 1:333–34, 344.

27. James, *Hawthorne,* 321.

Chapter Three: The Red Badge of Compromise

1. Melville, *Clarel: A Poem and Pilgrimage in the Holy Land,* ed. Walter E. Bezanson (New York: Hendricks House, 1960), 281, 157; Larry J. Reynolds, *European Revolutions and the American Literary Renaissance* (New Haven: Yale University Press, 1988), xii; David Morris Potter, *The Impending Crisis, 1848–1861,* ed. Don E. Fehrenbacher (New York: Harper and Row, 1976), 241–42.

2. Larry J. Reynolds, "The Scarlet Letter and Revolutions Abroad," *American Literature* 77 (1985): 44–67.

3. Duyckinck letters (George to Evert, March 5, 1848, and Evert to George, April 18, 1848), in Reynolds, *European Revolutions,* 10, 82; Bancroft (April 22, 1848), in Mark De Wolfe Howe, *The Life and Letters of George Bancroft* (New York: Scribners, 1908), 2:91; George Ticknor to George S. Hillard (July 17, 1848) in *Life, Letters, and Journals of George Ticknor* (Boston: J. R. Osgood, 1876), 2:234; Anon., "Revolutions Abroad," *New York Courier and Inquirer,* July 14, 1848, 1; Bancroft, in Howe, *Life and Letters,* 2:31, 33.

4. Anon., "The True Progress of Society," *The Biblical Repertory and Princeton Review* 24 (1852): 37, 21, 20, 17; [Francis Bowen], "Mill's Political Economy: Population and Property," *North American Review* 67 (1848): 377; and "French Ideas of Democracy and a Community of Goods," *North American Review,* 69 (1849): 281, 290, 298, 324, 279; Anon., "Societary Theories," *The American Review: A Whig Journal* 6 (1848): 645.

5. Anon., "Societary Theories," 633, 640–41, 637.

6. Reynolds, *European Revolutions,* 55; New York *Herald,* summer 1848, reprinted in *History of Woman Suffrage* (1881), ed. Elizabeth Cady Stanton, Susan B. Anthony, and Matilda Joslyn Gage (New York: Arno Reprints, 1969), 1:805; Anon., "The True Progress of Society," 34, 37; Rochester *Democrat,* Summer 1848, reprinted in *History of Woman Suffrage,* 1:804.

7. Matthiessen, *American Renaissance,* ix; Thoreau, *Journals,* ed. Bradford Torrey and Francis H. Allen (Boston: Houghton Mifflin, 1906), 3:208; Reynolds, *European Revolutions,* 169; Thoreau, *Journals,* 3:208, 210; Thoreau, *Walden: Or, Life in the Woods,* in *A Week on the Concord and Merrimack Rivers, Walden, The Maine Woods, Cape Cod,* ed. Robert F. Sayre (New York: Library of America, 1985), 504; Thoreau, *Journals,* 2:101–2.

8. Whitman, "Millet's Pictures—Last Items," "Europe, the 72nd and 73rd

Years of These States," and "To a Foil'd European Revolutionaire," in *Complete Poetry and Collected Prose,* ed. Justin Kaplan (New York: Library of America, 1982), 903–4, 133, 497–98; Gay Wilson Allen, *The Solitary Singer: A Critical Biography of Walt Whitman* (1955; New York: New York University Press, 1967), 212, quoting Whitman; Reynolds, *European Revolutions,* 172; Paul Zweig, *Walt Whitman: The Making of the Poet* (New York: Basic Books, 1984), p. 86.

9. Margaret Fuller Ossoli, *Memoirs,* ed. W. H. Channing, J. F. Clarke, and R. W. Emerson (Boston: Phillips, Samson, 1850), 2:235; and Fuller, *At Home and Abroad: Or, Things and Thoughts in America and Europe,* ed. A. B. Fuller (Boston: Crosby, Nichols, 1856), 305–6; and Fuller, New York *Tribune* suppl. (February 13, 1850), quoted in Reynolds, *European Revolutions,* 73; Ann Douglas, *The Feminization of American Culture* (New York: Knopf, 1977), 288–90.

10. Hawthorne, *Letters, 1843–1853,* ed. Thomas Woodson, L. Neal Smith, and Norman Holmes Pearson, in *Works,* Centenary Edition (Columbus: Ohio State University Press, 1985), 16:537; and *Life of Pierce,* 415 (my emphasis).

11. Hawthorne, *Life of Pierce,* 417.

12. James, *Hawthorne,* 372.

13. John Greenleaf Whittier, "The Kansas Emigrants," in *Complete Poetical Works* (Boston: Houghton Mifflin, 1894), 317; Lincoln, "Second Inaugural Address," in *Collected Works,* 8:333.

14. Melville, *Pierre,* 41, 240. See forthcoming essay by Liana Farber.

15. Bernard Bailyn, *The Ideological Origins of the American Revolution* (Cambridge, Mass.: Harvard University Press, 1967), 232–33; Edmund S. Morgan, *American Slavery, American Freedom: The Ordeal of Colonial Virginia* (New York: Norton, 1975), passim.

16. Melville, *Moby-Dick: or, The Whale,* in *Redburn, White-Jacket, Moby-Dick,* ed. G. Thomas Tanselle (New York: Library of America, 1983), 1258, 969.

17. Pierre Macherey, *A Theory of Literary Production,* trans. Geoffrey Wall (London: Routledge and Kegan Paul, 1978), passim.

18. Norman Mailer, *The Armies of the Night: History as a Novel, The Novel as History* (New York: NAL, 1968), 44; Thoreau, *Walden,* 577; Emerson, *Nature,* in *Essays and Lectures,* ed. Joel Porte (New York: Library of America, 1983), 10; Lansford Hastings, *Emigrant's Guide to Oregon and California* (Cincinnati, Ohio: G. Conclin, 1845), 133; [O'Sullivan], "The Great Nation of Futurity" in *United States Magazine and Democratic Review* 6 (1839): 427; Emerson, "Experience," in *Essays and Lectures,* 484–85.

19. Emerson, "The Fortune of the Republic," in *Works,* ed. J. E. Cabot (Boston: Houghton Mifflin, 1883), 11:416; [O'Sullivan], "Annexation," in *United States Magazine and Democratic Review* 17, n.s. (1845): 7 (my emphasis); Bancroft, "Oration, Delivered at the Commemoration of the Death of Andrew Jackson" (June 27, 1845), in *Literary and Historical Miscellanies* (New York: Harper, 1855), 446; William Gilpin (1846), quoted in Thomas L. Karnes, *William Gilpin: Western Nationalist* (Austin: University of Texas Press, 1970),

136; Charles Dana, *The Garden of the World: or, The Great West* (Boston: Wentworth, 1856), 13–14.

20. Thomas Jefferson, letter to William Short (April 13, 1820), in *Writings*, ed. Andrew A. Lipscomb et al. (Washington: Jefferson Memorial Association, 1903), 15:247.

21. Sacvan Bercovitch, "The Rites of Assent: Rhetoric, Ritual, and the Ideology of American Consensus," in *The American Self: Myth, Ideology, and Popular Culture*, ed. Sam B. Girgus (Albuquerque: University of New Mexico Press, 1981), 5–42.

22. Merrill D. Peterson, *The Great Triumvirate: Webster, Clay, and Calhoun* (Oxford: Oxford University Press, 1987); Daniel Webster, Henry Clay, "Speech to the Young Men at Albany" (May 28, 1851); "The Compromise Measures" (July 17, 1850); and "The Constitution and the Union" (March 7, 1850), in *Works* (Boston: Little, Brown, 1851), 2:580, 592; and 5:436, 361, 365; Henry Clay, "Speech on the Compromise Resolutions" (February 5 and 6, 1850), in *Works*, ed. Calvin Colton (New York: Putnam, 1904), 3:340; Mobile *Daily Register*, March 4, 1850, 2.

23. Thomas Hart Benton, speech of June 10, 1850; and William Seward, speech of March 11, 1850, in *The Compromise of 1850*, ed. Edwin C. Rozwenc (Boston: Heath, 1957), 21, 44–46; Horace Bushnell, "The Doctrine of Loyalty," in *Work and Play: or Literary Varieties* (New York: Scribners, 1864), 350–51; Webster, "The Constitution and the Union," 361, 324n, 365.

24. Webster's Standard American Dictionary, 3d ed.; Noah Webster, *American Dictionary of the English Language*, 1830, 1832; *American Dictionary*, 1841; and *American Dictionary . . . Revised and Enlarged*, 1850.

25. Emerson, "The Fugitive Slave Law" (1854), in *Works*, 11:216; Webster, "The Constitution and the Union," 325, 365; and "The Compromise Measures" (July 17, 1850), in *Works*, 5:437.

26. Hawthorne, *French and Italian Notebooks* (September, 1858), in *Works*, ed. Thomas Woodson, Centenary Edition (Columbus: Ohio State University Press, 1980), 14:433; Frank Preston Stearns, *The Life and Genius of Nathaniel Hawthorne* (Philadelphia: Lippincott, 1906), 261.

27. Sarah Hale, *Woman's Record . . . from "The Beginning" till A.D. 1850* (New York: Harper, 1853), xli–xliii, xxxv–xxxvii; Lincoln, "A House Divided," in *Collected Works*, 2:461 (my emphasis); Emerson, "John Brown," in *Works*, 11:251–52 ("Boston Speech").

28. James, *Hawthorne*, 412; Hawthorne, *Our Old Home*, in *Works*, Centenary Edition (Columbus: Ohio State University Press, 1970), 5:4.

29. James, *Hawthorne*, 425–26, 449; Hawthorne, preface to *The Marble Faun: Or, The Romance of Monte Beni*, in *Novels*, 854; and "Chiefly About War-Matters" (1862), in *Works*, Riverside Edition, ed. George Parsons Lathrop (Boston: Houghton Mifflin, 1883), 12:299.

30. Samuel Sherwood, *The Church's Flight into the Wilderness* (New York: S. Louder, 1776), 31; Thomas Paine, *Common Sense*, ed. Nelson F. Adkins (New York: Liberal Arts Press, 1953), 25–27; Jackson, "Second Annual Mes-

sage" (December 6, 1830), in *Antebellum American Culture: An Interpretive Anthology,* ed. David Brion Davis (Lexington: University Press of Kentucky, 1979), 241; Emerson, "The Method of Nature," in *Essays and Lectures,* 124.

31. Emerson, "The Fugitive Slave Law," 224–30 (my emphasis).

32. Bushnell, "The Growth of Law" (1843), in *Work and Play,* 100–101.

33. Julia Ward Howe, "Battle Hymn of the Republic," in *Parnassus,* ed. Ralph Waldo Emerson (Boston: J. R. Osgood, 1875), 230.

Chapter Four: The Paradoxes of Dissent

1. Charles Feidelson, Jr., *Symbolism and American Literature* (Chicago: University of Chicago Press, 1953), 15; John Irwin, *American Hieroglyphics: The Symbol of Egyptian Hieroglyphics in the American Renaissance* (New Haven, Conn.: Yale University Press, 1980), 245; Millicent Bell, "The Obliquity of Signs: *The Scarlet Letter,*" *Massachusetts Review* 23 (1982): 9–26.

2. *Oxford English Dictionary* (1986); Noah Webster, *American Dictionary* (1850).

3. [George Bailey Loring], review of *The Scarlet Letter, Massachusetts Quarterly Review* 12 (1850): 495–96, 498.

4. Richard Poirier, *The Renewal of Literature: Emersonian Reflections* (New York: Random House, 1988), 172, 47, quoting Emerson; Emerson, "Circles," in *Essays and Lectures,* 403–5, 408, 413.

5. Emerson, "The Individual" (1837), in *The Early Lectures,* ed. Stephen Whicher, Robert E. Spiller, and Wallace E. Williams (Cambridge, Mass.: Harvard University Press, 1964), 2:185–86.

6. Emerson, "Self-Reliance"; and "Circles," in *Essays and Lectures,* 262, 406; Emerson, "The Individual," in *Early Lectures,* 2:190–91.

7. Steven Lukes, *Individualism* (New York: Harper and Row, 1973), 16–24; Koenraad W. Swart, "Individualism in the Mid-Nineteenth Century," *Journal of the History of Ideas* 23 (1962): 84–88.

8. Anon., "The Course of Civilization," 214, 209.

9. F. Raymond, *Supplement au Dictionnaire de l'Academie Française,* 6th ed. (Paris: Libraire de Gustave Barbra, 1836); Pierre C. V. Boiste, *Dictionnaire Universel* (Bruxelles: J. P. Meline, 1835); M. P. Poitevin, *Nouveau Dictionnaire Universel* (Paris: C. Reinwald, 1860); M. Louis Barré, *Complement au Dictionnaire de l'Academie Française* (Paris: Firmin Didot, 1856); Karl Marx, *Grundrisse: Foundations of the Critique of Political Economy,* trans. M. Nicolous (New York: Random House, 1973), 158; John Stuart Mill, *On Liberty,* ed. Currin V. Shields (New York: Macmillan, 1956), 69, 80; Alexandre de Saint-Cherón, "Philosophie du droit," *Revue Encyclopédique* 53 (1831): 29; Yehoshua Arieli, *Individualism and Nationalism in American Ideology* (Cambridge, Mass.: Harvard University Press, 1964), 232–33; Pierre Leroux, "De la philosophie et du Christianisme," *Revue Encyclopédique* 55 (1832): 299–301; and "De l'individualisme et du socialisme" (1833), reprinted as appendix to David

Owen Evans, *Le socialisme romantique: Pierre Leroux et ses contemporains* (Paris, 1948), pp. 223–32.

10. Emerson, "The Young American," in *Essays and Lectures,* 217, 221; Hawthorne, "The Intelligence Office," in *Tales and Sketches,* 879.

11. Emerson, Journals R, J, and N (1841–43), in *Journals,* ed. William Gilman and J. E. Parsons (Cambridge, Mass.: Harvard University Press, 1970), 8:377, 160, 377, 249–51.

12. Emerson, "Experience"; and "The American Scholar," in *Essays and Lectures,* 485, 71, 53.

13. Emerson, Journal B (1836), in *Journals,* ed. Merton M. Sealts, Jr. (Cambridge, Mass.: Harvard University Press, 1965), 5:203; Journal E (1840), in *Journals,* ed. A. William Plumstead and Harrison Hayford (Cambridge, Mass.: Harvard University Press, 1969), 7:342; Journal A (1834), in *Journals,* ed. Alfred R. Ferguson (Cambridge, Mass.: Harvard University Press, 1964), 4:342; Journal E (1840), in *Journals,* 7:394–95; Journal U (1844), in *Journals,* ed. Ralph H. Orth and Alfred R. Ferguson (Cambridge, Mass.: Harvard University Press, 1971), 9:69; *Letters,* ed. Ralph L. Rusk (New York: Columbia University Press, 1939), "Lecture on the Times" (1841), in *Essays and Lectures,* 167.

14. John C. Gerber, "Emerson and the Political Economists," *New England Quarterly* 22 (1940): 352.

15. Emerson, Journal K (1842), *Journals,* 8:209; and "Fourierism and the Socialists" (1842), in *Essays and Lectures,* 1207; John L. Brown, "The Life of Paradise Anew," in *France and North America: Utopias and Utopians,* ed. Mathé Allain (Lafayette: University of Southern Louisiana Press, 1978), 77–79; Hawthorne, *The Blithedale Romance,* in *Novels,* 686, 830; Emerson, "New England Reformers," in *Essays and Lectures,* 591, 596, 591. I am indebted here to important studies in process on Emerson and individualism by Frank Albers, Anita Goldman, and Cyrus R. K. Patell.

16. Gerber, "Emerson and the Political Economists," 338; Emerson, *Journals* 9:366 (1846).

17. Emerson, "Historic Notes of Life and Letters in New England," in *Works* 10: 311; Journal RS (1849), in *Journals,* 11:77.

18. Emerson, Journal AZ (1849?), in *Journals,* 11:201; "Historic Notes," 308; "Wealth" (1851), in *Essays and Lectures,* 1000; "Circles"; and "The Young American," in *Essays and Lectures,* 413, 216, 213–14, 217, 226, 228.

19. Gerber, "Emerson and the Political Economists," 352; Emerson, "Natural Aristocracy" (1848), *Works,* 9:63; Journal GH (1847), in *Journals,* 10:154; "The Fortune of the Republic," in *Works,* 11:398–99; Journal CO (1851), in *Journals,* 11:397–98.

20. Jürgen Habermas, *The Philosophical Discourse of Modernity: Twelve Lectures,* trans. Frederick Lawrence (Cambridge, Mass.: MIT Press, 1987), 39.

21. John Jay Chapman, *Emerson and Other Essays* (New York: Scribners, 1898), 106, 107–8; Christopher Lasch, *The Culture of Narcissism: American Life in an Age of Diminishing Expectations* (New York: Norton, 1978); Harold

Bloom, "Mr. America," in *New York Review of Books* 31 (November 22, 1984): 23; Stanley Cavell, "Hope Against Hope," in *American Poetry Review* 1 (January–February, 1986): 13; Charles Feidelson, Jr., "The Scarlet Letter," in *Hawthorne Centenary Essays,* ed. Roy Harvey Pearce (Columbus: Ohio State University Press, 1964), 62–63.

22. Poirier, *The Renewal of Literature,* 151, 178, quoting William James, *Pragmatism* (1907).

23. Theodore Adorno, *Negative Dialectics,* trans. E. B. Ashton (New York: Seabury Press, 1973), 226; Emerson, Journal E (1842), in *Journals,* 7:483.

24. John Higham, *From Boundlessness to Consolidation: The Transformation of American Culture, 1848–1860* (Ann Arbor: William L. Clements Library, 1969).

25. Hans Blumenberg, *Work on Myth,* trans. Robert Wallace (Cambridge, Mass.: MIT Press, 1985), 221.

Postscript

1. Horatio Bridge, *Personal Recollections of Nathaniel Hawthorne* (New York: Harper, 1893), 112.

2. Stanley Fish, "Force," in *Doing What Comes Naturally: Change, Rhetoric, and the Practice of Theory in Literary and Legal Studies* (Durham, N.C.: Duke University Press, 1989), 518, 520 (italics altered).

3. Hawthorne, "Chiefly about War Matters," 319.

Index